FRIENDS: A POEM FOR EVERY DAY OF THE YEAR

FRIENDS: A POEM FOR EVERY DAY OF THE YEAR

EDITED BY *Jane McMorland Hunter*

BATSFORD

First published in the United Kingdom in 2019 by
Batsford
43 Great Ormond Street
London
WC1N 3HZ
An imprint of Pavilion Books Company Ltd

ISBN 978-1-84994-589-9

A CIP catalogue record for this book
is available from the British Library.

10 9 8 7 6 5 4 3 2 1

Reproduction by Rival Colour Ltd, UK
Printed and bound by Imak Offset, Turkey

This book can be ordered direct from the publisher
at www.pavilionbooks.com

Illustrations by Tatiana Boyko

CONTENTS

JANUARY 10
It is a Sweet Thing, Friendship

FEBRUARY 46
Let Us Hold Hands

MARCH 84
The Breath of Kindness

APRIL 122
The Spring is for Joy

MAY 160
Please Come Flying

JUNE 202
An Accord in All Things

JULY 240
Memories that Endure

AUGUST 282
With Cheerful Greeting

SEPTEMBER 324
Such Sweet Company

OCTOBER 364
In Sunshine and in Shade

NOVEMBER 402
A Little Laughter

DECEMBER 436
Winter is Deck'd with a Smile

INDEX OF FIRST LINES 478
INDEX OF POETS 488
ACKNOWLEDGEMENTS 493

To Louy and Matilda, with all my love.

ABOUT THE EDITOR

Jane McMorland Hunter has compiled six anthologies: *Favourite Poems of London*, *Favourite Poems of England*, *Classic Readings and Poems* and *A Nature Poem for Every Day of the Year* for Batsford and *Poems of the First World War* and *Favourite Poems* for The National Trust. She also writes gardening books and works as a gardener and as the Shop Scribe at Hatchards Bookshop in Piccadilly, compiling their annual catalogues.

Introduction

There are many different types of friends: old and new, those you see every day, others you might never see but whose contact is still important, and, ideally, lovers and married couples. This collection of poems is aimed at all of these people and more: children, students, families and people nearing the end of their lives who may have more ghostly friends than living ones. There are poems about friendship, poems you would give to a friend and one or two pieces of particularly poetic prose.

Throughout our lives we make, keep and, regrettably, lose friends. Old friends, as praised by Austin Dobson, may be the best, but there was a moment when they were new friends; first meetings, first friends and first loves are all important. At any stage of life, what is clear is that friends make most things better: William Wordsworth's description of skating, G. K. Chesterton's drunken outing and Robert Louis Stevenson's piratical adventures are all better because they are enjoyed in company. Even food tastes better with friends, as Ben Jonson's planning and Robert Herrick's lonely meal attest.

Our first friends are often our siblings, followed by school playmates and fellow scholars. It is at this point that love and friendship start to intertwine. Emily Brontë is clear on the difference between the two, describing one as an ephemeral wild briar rose and the other as an everlasting holly tree. Laura, in Thomas Moore's 'Temple to Friendship', confuses friendship and love when choosing a statue for her garden; how much more confusing are matters which involve real people. Sonnets by Elizabeth Barrett Browning, William Shakespeare and others describe feelings of love, but many of these could equally apply to our friends – do most of us not love our closest friends?

Marriage is, again ideally, a union of two friends. From Thomas Campion and Anne Bradstreet to William Barnes and Charles Jefferys, poets have extolled the virtues of friendship in marriage. Laurence Alma-Tadema points out that even if you fail to marry, a squirrel, a rabbit, a pony and a lamb will provide the companionship you need.

Animals are often our best friends, although some are more reliable than others; Elizabeth Barrett Browning's Flush is well known for his faithfulness but Tiger, Binkie and an unnamed watchdog also prove their worth at the hands of Jonathan Swift, Rudyard Kipling and Lord Byron. Cats have a more varied reputation, with Christopher Smart and others recognising that a cat's friendship is never quite as unquestioning as that of a dog. For other poets a falcon, a lamb, a tree and a hare are less likely soulmates (Thomas Wyatt, Sarah Josepha Hale, Christina Rossetti and William Cowper respectively).

Friendship between animals also exists, with the surprising pairing of a duck and a kangaroo courtesy of Edward Lear, and the charming faithfulness of a goldfinch who, in the mind of William Cowper, chooses to forsake freedom rather than desert his friend in their cage.

Memories of friends can be as important as friendship itself. Fleeting glimpses of happiness appear in Louis MacNeice's 'Sunlight on the Garden', and in Leigh Hunt's 'Rondeau' the memory of a single kiss outweighs all the trials and tribulations of old age. In some cases the memories can make the dead seem more alive than the living. Many poets write of lost friends and loves, either through death or misfortune. Whatever the cause, as Lord Tennyson writes, ''Tis better to have loved and lost, than never to have loved at all'.

As well as descriptions of friendships, this anthology also contains poems which one could give to a friend: Edward Thomas' 'Thaw', which sees the passing of winter, and John Drinkwater's 'Miracle', which welcomes spring. The pleasure of a walk in the countryside and the time to 'stand and stare' are things any friends would wish to share. W. B. Yeats gives us the perfect Christmas gesture of friendship, to spread one's dreams at another's feet.

Although this is an anthology of poetry, in each month there is a little prose. Essays by Francis Bacon, William Emerson and others were too moving to ignore. There are diaries, plays, passages from the Bible, and an extract from Charles Dickens' *The Pickwick Papers* which describe friendship in a poetical way even if they are not strictly poetry.

In many anthologies the order of the poems is governed by external factors: nature by the passing seasons, life by the passage of time itself. Here, apart from Valentine's, the famously exuberant spring and a few dates with personal connections, there was no such guide. It was impossible to place the poems so that they could be all things to all readers; my hope is that all will find some poems that pertain particularly to them whilst still being able to enjoy the others.

One of the most perceptive poems in this collection is by Edward Verrall Lucas, who rightly points out that often we cannot explain our choice of friends:

'We two are friends' tells everything.
Yet if you must know, this is why:
Because he is he and I am I.
Edward Verrall Lucas

JANUARY

It is a Sweet Thing, Friendship

Passages of the Poem, or Connected Therewith

LINES 62–77

It is a sweet thing, friendship, a dear balm,
A happy and auspicious bird of calm,
Which rides o'er life's ever tumultuous Ocean;
A God that broods o'er chaos in commotion;
A flower which fresh as Lapland roses are,
Lifts its bold head into the world's frore air,
And blooms most radiantly when others die,
Health, hope, and youth, and brief prosperity;
And with the light and odour of its bloom,
Shining within the dungeon and the tomb;
Whose coming is as light and music are
'Mid dissonance and gloom – a star
Which moves not 'mid the moving heavens alone –
A smile among dark frowns – a gentle tone
Among rude voices, a belovèd light,
A solitude, a refuge, a delight.

Percy Bysshe Shelley (1792–1822)

Since We Parted

Since we parted yester eve,
I do love thee, love, believe,
Twelve times dearer, twelve hours longer, –
One dream deeper, one night stronger,
One sun surer, – thus much more
Than I loved thee, love before.

Edward Bulwer-Lytton / Owen Meredith (1831–1891)

Brother and Sister

I cannot choose but think upon the time
When our two lives grew like two buds that kiss
At lightest thrill from the bee's swinging chime,
Because the one so near the other is.

He was the elder and a little man
Of forty inches, bound to show no dread,
And I the girl that puppy-like now ran,
Now lagged behind my brother's larger tread.

I held him wise, and when he talked to me
Of snakes and birds, and which God loved the best,
I thought his knowledge marked the boundary
Where men grew blind, though angels knew the rest.

If he said 'Hush!' I tried to hold my breath;
Wherever he said 'Come!' I stepped in faith.

George Eliot (1819–1880)

My Thanks

ACCOMPANYING MANUSCRIPTS PRESENTED TO A FRIEND, LINES 61–68

O friend beloved, whose curious skill
  Keeps bright the last year's leaves and flowers,
With warm, glad, summer thoughts to fill
  The cold, dark, winter hours!

Pressed on thy heart, the leaves I bring
  May well defy the wintry cold,
Until, in Heaven's eternal spring,
  Life's fairer ones unfold.

John Greenleaf Whittier (1807–1892)

The Oblation

Ask nothing more of me, sweet;
All I can give you I give.
Heart of my heart, were it more,
More would be laid at your feet:
Love that should help you to live,
Song that should spur you to soar.

All things were nothing to give,
Once to have sense of you more,
Touch you and taste of you, sweet,
Think you and breathe you and live,
Swept of your wings as they soar,
Trodden by chance of your feet.

I that have love and no more
Give you but love of you, sweet:
He that hath more, let him give;
He that hath wings, let him soar;
Mine is the heart at your feet
Here, that must love you to live.

Algernon Charles Swinburne (1837–1909)

XIV

FROM *SONNETS FROM THE PORTUGUESE*

If thou must love me, let it be for nought
Except for love's sake only. Do not say
'I love her for her smile – her look – her way
Of speaking gently – ; for a trick of thought
That falls in well with mine, and certes brought
A sense of pleasant ease on such a day' –
For these things in themselves, Beloved, may
Be changed, or change for thee, – and love so wrought,
May be unwrought so. Neither love me for
Thine own dear pity's wiping my cheeks dry, –
A creature might forget to weep, who bore
Thy comfort long, and lose thy love thereby!
But love me for love's sake, that evermore
Thou may'st love on, through love's eternity.

Elizabeth Barrett Browning (1806–1861)

The Reconcilement

Come, let us now resolve at last
  To live and love in quiet;
We'll tie the knot so very fast
  That Time shall ne'er untie it.

The truest joys they seldom prove
  Who free from quarrels live:
'Tis the most tender part of love
  Each other to forgive.

When least I seem'd concern'd, I took
  No pleasure nor no rest;
And when I feign'd an angry look,
  Alas! I loved you best.

Own but the same to me – you'll find
  How blest will be our fate.
O to be happy – to be kind –
  Sure never is too late!

John Sheffield, Duke of Buckingham (1648–1721)

If No One Ever Marries Me

If no one ever marries me –
  And I don't see why they should,
For nurse says I'm not pretty
  And I'm seldom very good –

If no one ever marries me
  I shan't mind very much;
I shall buy a squirrel in a cage,
  And a little rabbit hutch.

I shall have a cottage near a wood,
  And a pony all my own,
And a little lamb, quite clean and tame,
  That I can take to town.

And when I'm getting really old,
  At twenty eight or nine,
I shall buy a little orphan girl
  And bring her up as mine.

Laurence Alma-Tadema (c.1865–1940)

If I Could Tell You

Time will say nothing but I told you so,
Time only knows the price we have to pay;
If I could tell you I would let you know.

If we should weep when clowns put on their show,
If we should stumble when musicians play,
Time will say nothing but I told you so.

There are no fortunes to be told, although,
Because I love you more than I can say,
If I could tell you I would let you know.

The winds must come from somewhere when they blow,
There must be reasons why the leaves decay;
Time will say nothing but I told you so.

Perhaps the roses really want to grow,
The vision seriously intends to stay;
If I could tell you I would let you know.

Suppose the lions all get up and go,
And all the brooks and soldiers run away;
Will Time say nothing but I told you so?
If I could tell you I would let you know.

W. H. Auden (1907–1973)

Invitation to Love

Come when the nights are bright with stars
Or come when the moon is mellow;
Come when the sun his golden bars
Drops on the hay-field yellow.
Come in the twilight soft and gray,
Come in the night or come in the day,
Come, O love, whene'er you may,
And you are welcome, welcome.

You are sweet, O Love, dear Love,
You are soft as the nesting dove.
Come to my heart and bring it to rest
As the bird flies home to its welcome nest.

Come when my heart is full of grief
Or when my heart is merry;
Come with the falling of the leaf
Or with the redd'ning cherry.
Come when the year's first blossom blows,
Come when the summer gleams and glows,
Come with the winter's drifting snows,
And you are welcome, welcome.

Paul Laurence Dunbar (1872–1906)

To Mr I. L.

Of that short Roll of friends writ in my heart
  Which with thy name begins, since their depart,
Whether in the English Provinces they be,
  Or drinke of Po, Sequan, or Danubie,
There's none that sometime greets us not, and yet
  Your Trent is Lethe; that past, us you forget.
You doe not duties of Societies,
  If from th' embrace of a lov'd wife you rise,
View your fat Beasts, stretch'd Barns, and labour'd fields,
  Eat, play, ryde, take all joyes which all day yeelds,
And then againe to your embracements goe:
  Some houres on us your friends, and some bestow
Upon your Muse, else both wee shall repent,
  I that my love, she that her guifts on you are spent.

John Donne (1572–1631)

A Parting Song

'O MES AMIS! RAPELLEZ-VOUS QUELQUEFOIS MES VERS! MON AME Y EST EMPREINTÉ.' (MADAME DE STAËL)

When will ye think of me, my friends?
  When will ye think of me?
When the last red light, the farewell of day,
From the rock and the river is passing away –
When the air with a deepening hush is fraught,
And the heart grows tender with burdened thought
  Then let it be!

When will ye think of me, kind friends?
  When will ye think of me?
When the rose of the rich midsummer-time
Is filled with the hues of its glorious prime –
When ye gather its bloom, as in bright hours fled,
From the walks where my footsteps no more may tread –
  Then let it be!

When will ye think of me, sweet friends?
  When will ye think of me?
When the sudden tears o'erflow your eye
At the sound of some olden melody –
When ye hear the voice of a mountain-stream,
When ye feel the charm of a poet's dream –
  Then let it be!

Thus let my memory be with you, friends!
  Thus ever think of me!
Kindly and gently, but as of one
For whom 'tis well to be fled and gone –
As of a bird from a chain unbound,
As of a wanderer whose home is found –
  So let it be.

Felicia Hemans (1793–1835)

Song

Where the ash-tree weaves
Shadows over the river
And the willow's grey leaves
Shake and quiver –
Meet me and talk, love,
Down the grasshopper's baulk, love,
And then love forever.

There meet me and talk, love,
Of love's inward feelings
Where the clouds look like chalk, love,
And the huts and the shielings
Lie like love o'er the river
Here talk of love's feelings
And love on for ever.

Where the bee hums his ballads
By the river so near it
Round docks and wild salads
While all love to hear it,
We'll meet by the river
And by the old willow-pollards
Bid love live for ever.

John Clare (1793–1864)

The Wealth of Youth

FROM *DEDICATORY ODE*

The wealth of youth, we spent it well
  And decently, as very few can
And is it lost? I cannot tell:
  And what is more, I doubt if you can.

The question's very much too wide,
  And much too deep, and much too hollow,
And learned men on either side
  Use arguments I cannot follow.

They say that in the unchanging place,
  Where all we loved is always dear,
We meet our morning face to face
  And find at last our twentieth year ...

They say (and I am glad they say)
   It is so; and it may be so;
It may be just the other way,
   I cannot tell. But this I know:

From quiet homes and first beginning,
   Out to the undiscovered ends,
There's nothing worth the wear of winning,
   But laughter and the love of friends.

Hilaire Belloc (1870–1953)

Luckes, My Faire Falcon

Luckes, my faire falcon, and your fellowes all,
  How well plesaunt yt were your libertie!
Ye not forsake me that faire might ye befall.
  But they that sometyme lykt my companye,
Like lyse awaye from ded bodies thei crall.
  Loe, what a profe in light adversytie!
But ye, my birdes, I swear by all your belles,
Ye be my frynds, and so be but few elles.

Sir Thomas Wyatt (1503–1542)

A Sampler in a Farm House

FROM *THE DIARY OF FRANCIS KILVERT*

A little health,
A little wealth,
A little house and freedom,
And at the end
A little friend
And little cause to need him.

Anon

Sonnet

WRITTEN ON A BLANK PAGE IN SHAKESPEARE'S POEMS, FACING 'A LOVER'S COMPLAINT'

Bright star, would I were stedfast as thou art –
  Not in lone splendour hung aloft the night
And watching, with eternal lids apart,
  Like nature's patient, sleepless Eremite,
The moving waters at their priestlike task
  Of pure ablution round earth's human shores,
Or gazing on the new soft-fallen mask
  Of snow upon the mountains and the moors –
No – yet still stedfast, still unchangeable,
  Pillow'd upon my fair love's ripening breast,
To feel for ever its soft fall and swell,
  Awake for ever in a sweet unrest,
Still, still to hear her tender-taken breath,
  And so live ever – or else swoon to death.

John Keats (1795–1821)

The Human Touch

'Tis the human touch in this world that counts,
  The touch of your hand and mine,
Which means far more to the fainting heart
  Than shelter and bread and wine;
For shelter is gone when the night is o'er,
  And bread lasts only a day.
But the touch of the hand and the sound of the voice
  Sing on in the soul alway.

Spencer Michael Free (1856–1938)

Content and Rich

VERSES 1–11

I dwell in Grace's court,
  Enriched with Virtue's rights;
Faith guides my wit, Love leads my will,
  Hope all my mind delights.

In lowly vales I mount
  To pleasure's highest pitch;
My silly shroud true honour brings;
  My poor estate is rich.

My conscience is my crown,
  Contented thoughts my rest;
My heart is happy in itself;
  My bliss is in my breast.

Enough, I reckon wealth;
  A mean the surest lot,
That lies too high for base contempt,
  Too low for envy's shot.

My wishes are but few
  All easy to fulfil;
I make the limits of my power
  The bonds unto my will.

I have no hopes but one,
  Which is of heavenly reign;
Effects attained, or not desired,
  All lower hopes refrain.

I fear no care of coin;
  Well-doing is my wealth;
My mind to me an empire is,
  While grace affordeth health.

I clip high-climbing thoughts,
  The wings of swelling pride;
Their fall is worst that from the height
  Of greatest honour slide.

Sith sails of largest size
  The storm doth soonest tear;
I bear so low and small a sail
  As freeth me from fear.

I wrestle not with rage,
  While fury's flame doth burn;
It is in vain to stop the stream
  Until the tide doth turn.

But when the flame is out,
  And ebbing wrath doth end,
I turn a late enraged foe
  Into a quiet friend.

Robert Southwell (1561–1595)

Metaphor of Sunshine

  Heaven runs over
With sunshine which is poured into the brain
Of birds and poets, and kept for winter song;
And into flints to strike fire.

Thomas Lovell Beddoes (1803–1849)

Abou Ben Hadhem

Abou Ben Adhem (may his tribe increase!)
Awoke one night from a deep dream of peace,
And saw, within the moonlight in his room,
Making it rich, and like a lily in bloom,
An angel writing in a book of gold: –
Exceeding peace had made Ben Adhem bold,
And to the presence in the room he said,
'What writest thou?' – The vision rais'd its head,
And with a look made of all sweet accord,
Answer'd, 'The names of those who love the Lord.'
'And is mine one?' said Abou. 'Nay, not so,'
Replied the angel. Abou spoke more low,
But cheerily still; and said, 'I pray thee then,
Write me as one who loves his fellow-men.'

The angel wrote and vanish'd. The next night
It came again with a great wakening light,
And show'd the names whom love of God had bless'd,
And lo! Ben Adhem's name led all the rest.

Leigh Hunt (1784–1859)

The English are Frosty

FROM *THE WHITE CLIFFS*

The English are frosty
  When you're no kith or kin
Of theirs, but how they alter
  When once they take you in!
The kindest, the truest,
  The best friends ever known,
It's hard to remember
  How they froze you to a bone.
They showed me all London,
  Johnnie and his friends;
They took me to the country
  For long weekends;
I never was so happy,
  I never had such fun,
I stayed many weeks in England
  Instead of just one.

Alice Duer Miller (1874–1942)

Sonnet XXX

Love is not all: it is not meat or drink
Nor slumber nor a roof against the rain;
Nor yet a floating spar to men that sink
And rise and sink and rise and sink again;
Love cannot fill the thickened lung with breath,
Nor clean the blood, nor set the fractured bone;
Yet many a man is making friends with death
Even as I speak, for lack of love alone.
It may well be that in a difficult hour,
Pinned down by pain and moaning for release,
Or nagged by want past resolution's power,
I might be driven to sell your love for peace,
Or trade the memory of this night for food.
It may well be. I do not think I would.

Edna St Vincent Millay (1892–1950)

Claude to Eustace

FROM *AMOURS DU VOYAGE*, CANTO II, X

I am in love, meantime, you think; no doubt you
would think so.
I am in love, you say; with those letters, of course,
you would say so.
I am in love, you declare. I think not so; yet I grant you
It is a pleasure indeed to converse with this girl.
Oh, rare gift,
Rare felicity, this! she can talk in a rational way, can
Speak upon subjects that really are matters of mind and
of thinking,
Yet in perfection retain her simplicity; never, one moment,
Never, however you urge it, however you tempt her,
consents to
Step from ideas and fancies and loving sensations to
those vain
Conscious understandings that vex the minds of man-kind.
No, though she talk, it is music; her fingers desert not
the keys; 'tis
Song, though you hear in the song the articulate
vocables sounded,
Syllabled singly and sweetly the words of melodious
meaning.
I am in love, you say; I do not think so, exactly.

Arthur Hugh Clough (1819–1861)

Song

False though she be to me and Love,
  I'll ne'er pursue Revenge;
For still the Charmer I approve,
  Tho' I deplore her Change.

In Hours of Bliss we oft have met,
  They could not always last;
And though the present I regret,
  I'm grateful for the past.

William Congreve (1670–1729)

Daily Thoughts

JANUARY 26

A friend once won need never be lost, if we will be only trusty and true ourselves. Friends may part, not merely in body, but in spirit, for a while. In the bustle of business and the accidents of life, they may lose sight of each other for years; and more, they may begin to differ in their success in life, in their opinions, in their habits, and there may be, for a time, coldness and estrangement between them, but not for ever if each will be trusty and true. For then they will be like two ships who set sail at morning from the same port, and ere night-fall lose sight of each other, and go each on its own course and at its own pace for many days, through many storms and seas, and yet meet again, and find themselves lying side by side in the same haven when their long voyage is past.

Charles Kingsley (1819–1875)

Friendship

LINES 205–216

The noblest Friendship ever shewn
The Saviour's history makes known,
  Though some have turn'd and turn'd it;
And whether being craz'd or blind,
Or seeking with a bias'd mind,
  Have not, it seems, discern'd it.

Oh Friendship! if my soul forego
Thy dear delights while here below;
  To mortify and grieve me,
May I myself at last appear
Unworthy, base, and insincere,
  Or may my friend deceive me!

William Cowper (1731–1800)

Foure Things Make Us Happy Here

Health is the first good lent to men;
A gentle disposition then:
Next, to be rich by no by-wayes;
Lastly, with friends t'enjoy our dayes.

Robert Herrick (1591–1674)

Brave and Glorious

our journey was brief, it's true,
but brave and glorious.

split four ways now: three extant,
one dead.

those visionary days quite distant.
mortgages, cholesterol checks.

the occasional text
perhaps.

Joel Knight (1975–)

If I Can Stop One Heart From Breaking

If I can stop one Heart from breaking
I shall not live in vain
If I can ease one Life the Aching
Or cool one Pain

Or help one fainting Robin
Unto his Nest again
I shall not live in Vain.

Emily Dickinson (1830–1886)

Ballad

O sigh no more, love, sigh no more
Nor pine for earthly treasure
Who fears a shipwreck on the shore
Or meets despair with pleasure

Let not our wants our troubles prove
Although 'tis winter weather
Nor singly strive with what our love
Can better brave together

Thy love is proved thy worth is such
It cannot fail to bless me
If I loose thee I can't be rich
Nor poor if I possess thee

John Clare (1793–1864)

FEBRUARY

Let Us Hold Hands

Ice On the Highway

Seven buxom women abreast, and arm in arm,
  Trudge down the hill, tip-toed,
    And breathing warm;
They must perforce trudge thus, to keep upright
  On the glassy ice-bound road,
And they must get to market whether or no,
  Provisions running low
  With the nearing Saturday night,
While the lumbering van wherein they mostly ride
  Can nowise go:
Yet loud their laughter as they stagger and slide!

Thomas Hardy (1840–1928)

Sonnet CXVI

Let me not to the marriage of true minds
Admit impediments; love is not love
Which alters when it alteration finds,
Or bends with the remover to remove.
O, no, it is an ever-fixèd mark
That looks on tempests and is never shaken;
It is the star to every wand'ring bark,
Whose worth's unknown, although his height be taken.
Love's not Time's fool, though rosy lips and cheeks
Within his bending sickle's compass come;
Love alters not with his brief hours and weeks,
But bears it out even to the edge of doom.
If this be error and upon me proved,
I never writ, nor no man ever loved.

William Shakespeare (1564–1616)

To Mary Ann Lamb, the Author's Best Friend and Sister

If from my lips some angry accents fell,
Peevish complaint, or harsh reproof unkind,
'Twas but the error of a sickly mind
And troubled thoughts, clouding the purer well,
And waters clear, of Reason! And for me,
Let this my verse the poor atonement be –
My verse, which thou to praise wert e'er inclined
Too highly, and with a painful eye to see
No blemish. Thou to me didst ever show
Kindest affection, and would oft-times lend
An ear to the desponding love-sick lay,
Weeping my sorrows with me, who repay
But ill the mighty debt of love I owe,
Mary, to thee, my sister, and my friend.

Charles Lamb (1775–1834)

Hope

'Hope' is the thing with feathers –
That perches in the soul –
And sings the tune without the words –
And never stops – at all –

And sweetest – in the Gale – is heard –
And sore must be the storm –
That could abash the little Bird
That kept so many warm –

I've heard it in the chillest land –
And on the strangest Sea –
Yet, never, in Extremity,
It asked a crumb – of Me.

Emily Dickinson (1830–1886)

The Duck and the Kangaroo

Said the Duck to the Kangaroo,
  'Good gracious! how you hop!
Over the fields and the water too,
  As if you never would stop!
My life is a bore in this nasty pond,
And I long to go out in the world beyond!
  I wish I could hop like you!'
  Said the Duck to the Kangaroo.

'Please give me a ride on your back!'
  Said the Duck to the Kangaroo.
'I would sit quite still, and say nothing but "Quack,"
  The whole of the long day through!
And we'd go to the Dee, and the Jelly Bo Lee,
Over the land, and over the sea; –
  Please take me a ride! O do!'
  Said the Duck to the Kangaroo.

Said the Kangaroo to the Duck,
  'This requires some little reflection;
Perhaps on the whole it might bring me luck,
  And there seems but one objection,
Which is, if you'll let me speak so bold,
Your feet are unpleasantly wet and cold,
  And would probably give me the
roo-matiz!' said the Kangaroo.

Said the Duck, 'As I sate on the rocks,
  I have thought over that completely,
And I bought four pairs of worsted socks
  Which fit my web-feet neatly.
And to keep out the cold I've bought a cloak,
And every day a cigar I'll smoke,
  All to follow my own dear true
  Love of a Kangaroo!'

Said the Kangaroo, 'I'm ready!
  All in the moonlight pale;
But to balance me well, dear Duck, sit steady!
  And quite at the end of my tail!'
So away they went with a hop and a bound,
And they hopped the whole world three times round;
  And who so happy, – O who,
  As the Duck and the Kangaroo?

Edward Lear (1812–1888)

Friendship

LINES 25–46

For when two soules are chang'd and mixed soe,
It is what they and none but they can doe
And this is friendship, that abstracted flame
Which creeping mortals know not how to name.
All Love is sacred, and the marriage ty
Hath much of Honour and divinity.
But Lust, design, or some unworthy ends
May mingle there, which are despis'd by friends.
Passions hath violent extreams, and thus
All oppositions are contiguous.
So when the end is serv'd the Love will bate,
If friendship make it not more fortunate:
Friendship that Love's elixir, that pure fire
Which burns the clearer 'cause it burns the higher.
For Love, like earthly fires (which will decay
If the materiall fuell be away)
Is with offensive smoake accompany'd,
And by resistance only is supply'd.
But friendship, like the fiery element,
With its own heat and nourishment content,
(Where neither hurt, nor smoke, nor noise is made)
Scorns the assistance of a forein ayde.

Katherine Philips (1632–1664)

A True Friend

FROM *ON FRIENDSHIP*

A principal fruit of friendship, is the ease and discharge of the fullness and swellings of the heart, which passions of all kinds do cause and induce. We know diseases of stoppings and suffocations are the most dangerous in the body; and it is not much otherwise in the mind; you may take sarza to open the liver, steel to open the spleen, flowers of sulphur for the lungs, castoreum for the brain; but no receipt openeth the heart, but a true friend; to whom you may impart griefs, joys, fears, hopes, suspicions, counsels, and whatsoever lieth upon the heart to oppress it, in a kind of civil shrift or confession.

Francis Bacon (1561–1626)

Sonnet

FROM *LA VITA NUOVA*

Love and the gentle heart are one same thing,
  Even as the wise man in his ditty saith:
  Each, of itself, would be such life in death
As rational soul bereft of reasoning.
'Tis Nature makes them when she loves: a king
  Love is, whose palace where he sojourneth
  Is called the Heart; there draws he quiet breath
At first, with brief or longer slumbering.
Then beauty seen in virtuous womankind
  Will make the eyes desire, and through the heart
    Send the desiring of the eyes again;
Where often it abides so long enshrin'd
  That Love at length out of his sleep will start.
    And women feel the same for worthy men.

Dante Alighieri (1265–1321)
Translated by Dante Gabriel Rossetti (1828–1882)

CXIX

FROM *IN MEMORIAM A. H. H.*

Doors, where my heart was used to beat
  So quickly, not as one that weeps
  I come once more; the city sleeps;
I smell the meadow in the street;

I hear a chirp of birds; I see
  Betwixt the black fronts long-withdrawn
  A light-blue lane of early dawn,
And think of early days and thee,

And bless thee, for thy lips are bland,
  And bright the friendship of thine eye;
  And in my thoughts with scarce a sigh
I take the pressure of thine hand.

Alfred, Lord Tennyson (1809–1892)

In a Bath Teashop

'Let us not speak, for the love we bear one another –
  Let us hold hands and look.'
She, such a very ordinary little woman;
  He, such a thumping crook;
But both, for a moment, little lower than the angels
  In the teashop's ingle-nook.

John Betjeman (1906–1984)

Song

The girl I love is flesh and blood
  With face and form of fairest clay
Straight as the firdale in the wood
  And lovely as a first spring day

The girl I love's a lovely girl
  Bonny and young in every feature
Richer than flowers and strings o' pearl
  A handsome and delightful creature

She's born to grace the realms above
  Where we shall both be seen together
And sweet and fair the maid I love
  As rose trees are in summer weather

O bonny straight and fair is she
  I wish we both lived close together
Like as the acorns on the tree
  Or foxglove-bell in summer weather

Come to me love and let us dwell
  Where oak-trees cluster all together
I'll gaze upon thy bosom's swell
  And love yes love thee then forever

Her face is like another's face
  As white another's skin may prove
But no one else could fill her place
  If banished from the maid I love

John Clare (1793–1864)

To His Familiar Frend

No image carved with coonnying hand, no cloth
  of purple dye,
No precious weight of metall bright, no silver
  plate gyve I:
Such gear allures not hevenly herts: such gifts
  no grace they bring:
I lo, that know your minde, will send none such,
  what then? Nothing.

Nicholas Grimald (1519–1562)

Bill and Joe

Come, dear old comrade, you and I
Will steal an hour from days gone by,
The shining days when life was new,
And all was bright with morning dew,
The lusty days of long ago,
When you were Bill and I was Joe.

Your name may flaunt a titled trail
Proud as a cockerel's rainbow tail,
And mine as brief appendix wear
As Tam O'Shanter's luckless mare;
To-day, old friend, remember still
That I am Joe and you are Bill.

You've won the great world's envied prize,
And grand you look in people's eyes,
With H O N. and L. L. D.
In big brave letters, fair to see, –
Your fist, old fellow! off they go! –
How are you, Bill? How are you, Joe?

You've worn the judge's ermined robe;
You've taught your name to half the globe;
You've sung mankind a deathless strain;
You've made the dead past live again:
The world may call you what it will,
But you and I are Joe and Bill.

The chaffing young folks stare and say
'See those old buffers, bent and gray, –
They talk like fellows in their teens
Mad, poor old boys! That's what it means,' –
And shake their heads; they little know
The throbbing hearts of Bill and Joe! –

How Bill forgets his hour of pride,
While Joe sits smiling at his side;
How Joe, in spite of time's disguise,
Finds the old schoolmate in his eyes, –
Those calm, stern eyes that melt and fill
As Joe looks fondly up at Bill.

Ah, pensive scholar, what is fame?
A fitful tongue of leaping flame;
A giddy whirlwind's fickle gust,
That lifts a pinch of mortal dust;
A few swift years, and who can show
Which dust was Bill and which was Joe?

The weary idol takes his stand,
Holds out his bruised and aching hand,
While gaping thousands come and go, –
How vain it seems, this empty show!
Till all at once his pulses thrill; –
'Tis poor old Joe's 'God bless you, Bill!'

And shall we breathe in happier spheres
The names that pleased our mortal ears;
In some sweet lull of harp and song
For earth-born spirits none too long,
Just whispering of the world below
Where this was Bill and that was Joe?

No matter; while our home is here
No sounding name is half so dear;
When fades at length our lingering day,
Who cares what pompous tombstones say?
Read on the hearts that love us still,
Hic jacet Joe. *Hic jacet* Bill.

Oliver Wendell Holmes (1809–1894)

Phillis Inamorata

Come, be my Valentine!
I'll gather eglantine,
Cowslips and sops-in-wine,
  With fragrant roses.
Down by thy Phillis sit,
She will white lilies get,
And daffadilies fit
  To make thee posies.

I have a milk-white lamb,
New-taken from the dam,
It comes where'er I am
  When I call 'Willy:'
I have a wanton kid
Under my apron hid,
A colt that ne'er was rid,
  A pretty filly.

I bear in sign of love
A sparrow in my glove,
And in my breast a dove,
  This shall be all thine:
Besides of sheep a flock,
Which yieldeth many a lock,
And this shall be thy stock:
  Come, be my Valentine!

Lancelot Andrewes, Bishop of Winchester (1555–1626)

Music

Let me go where'er I will
I hear a sky-born music still;
It sounds from all things old,
It sounds from all things young,
From all that's fair, from all that's foul,
Peals out a cheerful song.

It is not only in the rose,
It is not only in the bird,
Not only when the rainbow glows,
Nor in the song of woman heard,
But in the darkest, meanest things
There alway, alway, something sings.

'Tis not in the high stars alone,
Nor in the cup of budding flowers,
Nor in the redbreast's mellow tones,
Nor in the bow that smiles in showers,
But in the mud and scum of things
There alway, alway, something sings.

Ralph Waldo Emerson (1803–1882)

Sonnet

Why art thou silent! Is thy love a plant
Of such weak fibre that the treacherous air
Of absence withers what was once so fair?
Is there no debt to pay, no boon to grant?
Yet have my thoughts for thee been vigilant –
Bound to thy service with unceasing care,
The mind's least generous wish a mendicant
For nought but what thy happiness could spare.
Speak – though this soft warm heart, once
  free to hold
A thousand tender pleasures, thine and mine,
Be left more desolate, more dreary cold
Than a forsaken bird's-nest filled with snow
'Mid its own bush of leafless eglantine –
Speak, that my torturing doubts their end may know!

William Wordsworth (1770–1850)

17 FEBRUARY

Love is What it is

Love is a circle that doth restlesse move
In the same sweet eternity of love.

Robert Herrick (1591–1674)

When You are Old

When you are old and grey and full of sleep,
And nodding by the fire, take down this book,
And slowly read, and dream of the soft look
Your eyes had once, and of their shadows deep;

How many loved your moments of glad grace,
And loved your beauty with love false or true,
But one man loved the pilgrim soul in you,
And loved the sorrows of your changing face;

And bending down beside the glowing bars,
Murmur, a little sadly, how Love fled
And paced upon the mountains overhead
And hid his face amid a crowd of stars.

W. B. Yeats (1865–1939)

The Fire of Drift-Wood

DEVEREUX FARM NEAR MARBLEHEAD

We sat within the farm-house old,
  Whose windows, looking o'er the bay,
Gave to the sea-breeze damp and cold,
  An easy entrance, night and day.

Not far away we saw the port,
  The strange, old-fashioned, silent town,
The lighthouse, the dismantled fort,
  The wooden houses, quaint and brown.

We sat and talked until the night,
  Descending, filled the little room;
Our faces faded from the sight,
  Our voices only broke the gloom.

We spake of many a vanished scene,
  Of what we once had thought and said,
Of what had been, and might have been,
  And who was changed, and who was dead;

And all that fills the hearts of friends,
  When first they feel, with secret pain,
Their lives thenceforth have separate ends,
  And never can be one again;

The first slight swerving of the heart,
  That words are powerless to express,
And leave it still unsaid in part,
  Or say it in too great excess.

The very tones in which we spake
  Had something strange, I could but mark;
The leaves of memory seemed to make
  A mournful rustling in the dark.

Oft died the words upon our lips,
  As suddenly, from out the fire
Built of the wreck of stranded ships,
  The flames would leap and then expire.

And, as their splendour flashed and failed,
  We thought of wrecks upon the main,
Of ships dismasted, that were hailed
  And sent no answer back again.

The windows, rattling in their frames,
  The ocean, roaring up the beach,
The gusty blast, the bickering flames,
  All mingled vaguely in our speech;

Until they made themselves a part
  Of fancies floating through the brain,
The long-lost ventures of the heart,
  That send no answers back again.

O flames that glowed! O hearts that yearned!
  They were indeed too much akin,
The drift-wood fire without that burned,
  The thoughts that burned and glowed within.

Henry Wadsworth Longfellow (1807–1882)

To F C.

20TH FEBRUARY 1875

Fast falls the snow, O lady mine,
Sprinkling the lawn with crystals fine,
But by the gods we won't repine
  While we're together,
We'll chat and rhyme and kiss and dine,
  Defying weather.

So stir the fire and pour the wine,
And let those sea-green eyes divine
Pour their love-madness into mine:
  I don't care whether
'Tis snow or sun or rain or shine
  If we're together.

Mortimer Collins (1827–1876)

Fidelis

You have taken back the promise
  That you spoke so long ago;
Taken back the heart you gave me–
  I must even let it go.
Where Love once has breathed, Pride dieth,
  So I struggled, but in vain,
First to keep the links together,
  Then to piece the broken chain.

But it might not be – so freely
  All your friendship I restore,
And the heart that I had taken
  As my own forevermore.
No shade of reproach shall touch you,
  Dread no more a claim from me–
But I will not have you fancy
  That I count myself as free.

I am bound by the old promise;
  What can break that golden chain?
Not even the words that you have spoken,
  Or the sharpness of my pain:
Do you think, because you fail me
  And draw back your hand today,
That from out the heart I gave you
  My strong love can fade away?

It will live. No eyes may see it;
  In my soul it will lie deep,
Hidden from all; but I shall feel it
  Often stirring in its sleep.
So remember that the friendship
  Which you now think poor and vain,
Will endure in hope and patience,
  Till you ask for it again.

Perhaps in some long twilight hour,
  Like those we have known of old,
When past shadows gather round you,
  And your present friends grow cold,
You may stretch your hands out towards me–
  Ah! You will – I know not when–
I shall nurse my love and keep it
Faithfully, for you, till then.

Adelaide Proctor (1825–1864)

Lay Morals

FROM CHAPTER IV

So long as we love we serve; so long as we are loved by others, I would almost say that we are indispensable; and no man is useless while he has a friend. The true services of life are inestimable in money, and are never paid. Kind words and caresses, high and wise thoughts, humane designs, tender behaviour to the weak and suffering, and all the charities of man's existence, are neither bought nor sold.

Robert Louis Stevenson (1850–1894)

XLI

FROM *SONNETS FROM THE PORTUGUESE*

I thank all who have loved me in their hearts,
With thanks and love from mine. Deep thanks to all
Who paused a little near the prison-wall
To hear my music in its louder parts
Ere they went onward, each one, to the mart's
Or temple's occupation, beyond call.
But thou, who, in my voice's sink and fall,
When the sob took it, thy divinest Art's
Own instrument, didst drop down at thy foot
To hearken what I said between my tears, ...
Instruct me how to thank thee! – Oh, to shoot
My soul's full meaning into future years, –
That they should lend it utterance, and salute
Love that endures, with Life that disappears! –

Elizabeth Barrett Browning (1806–1861)

Friendship

Friendship needs no studied phrases,
  Polished face, or winning wiles;
Friendship deals no lavish praises,
  Friendship dons no surface smiles.

Friendship follows Nature's diction,
  Shuns the blandishments of Art,
Boldly severs truth from fiction,
  Speaks the language of the heart.

Friendship favours no condition,
  Scorns a narrow-minded creed,
Lovingly fulfills its mission,
  Be it word or be it deed.

Friendship cheers the faint and weary,
  Makes the timid spirit brave,
Warns the erring, lights the dreary,
  Smooths the passage to the grave.

Friendship – pure, unselfish friendship,
  All through life's allotted span,
Nurtures, strengthens, widens, lengthens,
  Man's relationship with man.

Anon

To Jane: The Invitation

Best and brightest, come away!
Fairer far than this fair Day,
Which, like thee to those in sorrow,
Comes to bid a sweet good-morrow
To the rough Year just awake
In its cradle on the brake
The brightest hour of unborn Spring,
Through the winter wandering,
Found, it seems, the halcyon Morn
To hoar February born.
Bending from Heaven, in azure mirth,
It kiss'd the forehead of the Earth,
And smiled upon the silent sea,
And bade the frozen streams be free,
And waked to music all their fountains,
And breathed upon the frozen mountains,
And like a prophetess of May
Strewed flowers upon the barren way,
Making the wintry world appear
Like one on whom thou smilest, dear
Away, away, from men and towns,
To the wild wood and the downs –
To the silent wilderness
Where the soul need not repress
Its music lest it should not find
An echo in another's mind,
While the touch of Nature's art
Harmonizes heart to heart.
I leave this notice on my door

For each accustomed visitor: –
'I am gone into the fields
To take what this sweet hour yields; –
Reflection, you may come to-morrow,
Sit by the fireside with Sorrow. –
You with the unpaid bill, Despair, –
You, tiresome verse-reciter, Care, –
I will pay you in the grave, –
Death will listen to your stave.
Expectation too, be off!
To-day is for itself enough;
Hope, in pity mock not Woe
With smiles, nor follow where I go;
Long having lived on thy sweet food,
At length I find one moment's good
After long pain – with all your love,
That you never told me of.'

Radiant Sister of the Day,
Awake! Arise! And come away!
To the wild woods and the plains,
And the pools where winter rains
Image all their roof of leaves,
Where the pine its garland weaves
Of sapless green and ivy dun
Round stems that never kiss the sun;
Where the lawns and pastures be,
And the sandhills of the sea; –

Where the melting hoar-frost wets
The daisy-star that never sets,
And wind-flowers, and violets,
Which yet join not scent to hue,
Crown the pale year weak and new;
When the night is left behind
In the deep east, dun and blind,
And the blue noon is over us,
And the multitudinous
Billows murmur at our feet,
Where the earth and ocean meet,
And all things seem only one
In the universal sun.

Percy Bysshe Shelley (1792–1822)

No Labor-saving Machine

No labor-saving machine,
Nor discovery have I made,
Nor will I be able to leave behind me any wealthy
  bequest to found a hospital or library,
Nor reminiscence of any deed of courage for America,
Nor literary success nor intellect, nor book for the
  book-shelf,
But a few carols vibrating through the air I leave,
For comrades and lovers.

Walt Whitman (1819–1892)

The Miracle

Come, sweetheart, listen, for I have a thing
Most wonderful to tell you – news of spring.

Albeit winter still is in the air,
And the earth troubled, and the branches bare,

Yet down the fields to-day I saw her pass –
The spring – her feet went shining through the grass.

She touched the ragged hedgerows – I have seen
Her finger-prints, most delicately green;

And she has whispered to the crocus leaves,
And to the garrulous sparrows in the eaves.

Swiftly she passed and shyly, and her fair
Young face was hidden in her cloudy hair.

She would not stay, her season is not yet,
But she has reawakened, and has set

The sap of all the world astir, and rent
Once more the shadows of our discontent.

Triumphant news – a miracle I sing –
The everlasting miracle of spring.

John Drinkwater (1882–1937)

Thaw

Over the land freckled with snow half-thawed
The speculating rooks at their nests cawed
And saw from elm-tops, delicate as flower of grass,
What we below could not see, Winter pass.

Edward Thomas (1878–1917)

We Talked As Girls Do

We talked as Girls do –
Fond, and late –
We speculated fair, on every subject, but the Grave –
Of ours, none affair –

We handled Destinies, as cool –
As we – Disposers – be –
And God, a Quiet Party
To our Authority –

But fondest, dwelt upon Ourself
As we eventual – be –
When Girls to Women, softly raised
We – occupy – Degree –

We parted with a contract
To cherish, and to write
But Heaven made both, impossible
Before another night.

Emily Dickinson (1830–1886)

MARCH

The Breath of Kindness

Surly Winter Passes Off

FROM *THE SEASONS: SPRING*

And see where surly Winter passes off,
Far to the north, and calls his ruffian blasts:
His blasts obey, and quit the howling hill,
The shatter'd forest, and the ravaged vale;
While softer gales succeed, at whose kind touch,
Dissolving snows in livid torrents lost,
The mountains lift their green heads to the sky.

James Thomson (1700–1748)

The Year's at the Spring

FROM *PIPPA PASSES*

The year's at the spring,
And day's at the morn;
Morning's at seven;
The hill-side's dew-pearled;
The lark's on the wing;
The snail's on the thorn;
God's in His heaven –
All's right with the world!

Robert Browning (1812–1889)

Life

Let me but live my life from year to year,
  With forward face and unreluctant soul;
  Not hurrying to, nor turning from the goal;
Not mourning for the things that disappear
In the dim past, nor holding back in fear
  From what the future veils; but with a whole
  And happy heart, that pays its toll
To Youth and Age, and travels on with cheer.

So let the way wind up the hill or down,
  O'er rough or smooth, the journey will be joy:
  Still seeking what I sought when but a boy,
New friendship, high adventure, and a crown,
My heart will keep the courage of the quest,
And hope the road's last turn will be the best.

Henry van Dyke (1852–1933)

Friends – With a Difference

O, one I need to love me,
  – And one to understand,
And one to soar above me.
  – And one to clasp my hand,

And one to make me slumber,
  – And one to bid me strive,
But seven's the sacred number
  – That keeps the soul alive.

And first and last of seven,
  – And all the world and more,
Is she I need in Heaven,
  – And may not need before.

Mary Coleridge (1861–1907)

The Word

My friend, my bonny friend, when we are old,
  And hand in hand go tottering down the hill,
May we be rich in love's refinèd gold,
  May love's gold coin be current with us still.

May love be sweeter for the vanished days,
  And your most perfect beauty still as dear
As when your troubled finger stood at gaze
  In the dear March of a most sacred year.

May what we are be all we might have been,
  And that potential, perfect, O my friend,
And may there still be many sheafs to glean
  In our love's acre, comrade, till the end.

And may we find, when ended is the page
Death but a tavern on our pilgrimage.

John Masefield (1878–1967)

Claude to Eustace

FROM *AMOURS DU VOYAGE*, CANTO II, XI

There are two different kinds, I believe, of human
attraction:
One which simply disturbs, unsettles, and makes
you uneasy,
And another that poises, retains, and fixes and holds you.
I have no doubt, for myself, in giving my voice for
the latter.
I do not wish to be moved, but growing where I was
growing,
There more truly to grow, to live where as yet
I had languished.
I do not like being moved: for the will is excited; and action
Is a most dangerous thing; I tremble for something
factitious,
Some malpractice of heart and illegitimate process;
We are so prone to these things, with our terrible
notions of duty.

Arthur Hugh Clough (1819–1861)

Friends

You ask me 'why I like him.' Nay,
I cannot; nay, I would not, say.
I think it vile to pigeonhole
The pros and cons of a kindred soul.

You 'wonder he should be my friend.'
But then why should you comprehend?
Thank God for this – a new – surprise:
My eyes, remember, are not your eyes.

Cherish this one small mystery;
And marvel not that love can be
'In spite of all his many flaws.'
In spite? Supposing I said 'Because.'

A truce, a truce to questioning:
'We two are friends' tells everything.
Yet if you must know, this is why:
Because he is he and I am I.

Edward Verrall Lucas (1868–1938)

Lies About Love

We are a liars, because
the truth of yesterday becomes a lie to-morrow,
whereas letters are fixed,
and we live by the letter of truth.

The love I feel for my friend, this year,
is different from the love I felt last year.
If it were not so, it would be a lie.
Yet we re-iterate love! love!
as if it were a coin with a fixed value
instead of a flower that dies, and opens a different bud.

D. H. Lawrence (1885–1930)

LXV

FROM *IN MEMORIAM A. H. H.*

Sweet soul, do with me as thou wilt;
  I lull a fancy trouble-tost
  With 'Love's too precious to be lost,
A little grain shall not be spilt.'

And in that solace can I sing,
  Till out of painful phases wrought
  There flutters up a happy thought,
Self-balanced on a lightsome wing:

Since we deserved the name of friends,
  And thine effect so lives in me,
  A part of mine may live in thee
And move thee on to noble ends.

Alfred, Lord Tennyson (1809–1892)

The Lover Pleads With His Friend

Though you are in your shining days,
Voices among the crowd
And new friends busy with your praise,
Be not unkind or proud,
But think about old friends the most:
Time's bitter flood will rise,
Your beauty perish and be lost
For all eyes but these eyes.

W. B. Yeats (1865–1939)

A Letter

LINES 1–32

I ne'r was drest in Forms; nor can I bend
My pen to flatter any, nor commend.
Unless desert or honour do present
Unto my verse a worthy argument.

You are my friend, and in that word to me
Stand blazon'd in your noblest Heraldry;
That style presents you full, and does relate
The bounty of your love, and my own fate,
Both which conspir'd to make me yours. A choice
Which needs must in the giddy peoples voice,
That onely judge the outside, and like apes
Play with our names, and comment on our shapes,
Appear too light: but it lies you upon
To justifie the disproportion.

Truth be my record, I durst not presume
To seek to you, 'twas you that did assume
Me to your bosom. Wherein you subdu'd
One that can serve you, though ne're could intrude
Upon great titles; nor knows how t'invade
Acquaintance: Like such as are onely paid
With great mens smiles; if that the passant Lord
Let fall a forc't salute, or but afford
The Nod Regardant. It was test enough
For me, you ne're did find such servile stuff
Couch't in my temper; I can freely say,
I do not love you in that common way
For which Great Ones are lov'd in this false time:
I have no wish to gain, nor will to climbe;
I cannot pawn my freedom, nor out-live
My liberty for all that you can give.
And sure you may retain good cheap such friends,
Who not your fortune make, but you, their ends.

Henry King, Bishop of Chichester (1592–1669)

Retirement

LINES 725–42

Friends, not adopted with a school-boy's haste,
But chosen with a nice discerning taste,
Well-born, well-disciplin'd, who, plac'd apart
From vulgar minds, have honour much at heart,
And, though the world may think th' ingredients odd,
The love of virtue, and the fear of God!
Such friends prevent what else would soon succeed,
A temper rustic as the life we lead,
And keep the polish of the manners clean,
As their's who bustle in the busiest scene;
For solitude, however some may rave,
Seeming a sanctuary, proves a grave,
A sepulchre in which the living lie,
Where all good qualities grow sick and die.
I praise the Frenchman, his remark was shrewd –
How sweet, how passing sweet, is solitude!
But grant me still a friend in my retreat,
Whom I may whisper – solitude is sweet.

William Cowper (1731–1800)

Friendship

FROM *A LIFE FOR A LIFE*

Oh, the comfort – the inexpressible comfort of
feeling safe with a person,
Having neither to weigh thoughts,
Nor measure words – but pouring them
All right out – just as they are –
Chaff and grain together –
Certain that a faithful hand will
Take and sift them –
Keep what is worth keeping –
And with the breath of kindness
Blow the rest away.

Dinah Craik (1826–1887)

To Richard Watson Gilder

Old friends are best! And so to you
  Again I send, in closer throng,
  No unfamiliar shapes of song,
But those that once you liked and knew.

You surely will not do them wrong;
  For are you not an old friend, too? –
        Old friends are best.

Old books, old wine, old Nankin blue; –
  All things, in short, to which belong
  The charm, the grace that Time makes strong, –
All these I prize, but (*entre nous*)
        Old friends are best!

Austin Dobson (1840–1921)

Written in March

WHILE RESTING ON THE BRIDGE AT THE FOOT
OF BROTHER'S WATER

The Cock is crowing,
The stream is flowing,
The small birds twitter,
The lake doth glitter
The green field sleeps in the sun;
The oldest and youngest
Are at work with the strongest;
The cattle are grazing,
Their heads never raising;
There are forty feeding like one!

Like an army defeated
The snow hath retreated,
And now doth fare ill
On the top of the bare hill;
The ploughboy is whooping – anon-anon:
There's joy in the mountains;
There's life in the fountains;
Small clouds are sailing,
Blue sky prevailing;
The rain is over and gone!

William Wordsworth (1770–1850)

To Jennie

Good-bye! a kind good-bye,
I bid you now, my friend,
And though 'tis sad to speak the word,
To destiny I bend
And though it be decreed by Fate
That we ne'er meet again,
Your image, graven on my heart,
Forever shall remain.
Aye, in my heart thoult have a place,
Among the friends held dear, –
Nor shall the hand of Time efface
The memories written there.
Goodbye,
S. L. C.

Mark Twain (1835–1910)

17 MARCH

True Happiness

FROM *CYNTHIA'S REVELS*, ACT III, SCENE II

It is the pride of Arete to grace
Her studious lovers; and, in scorn of time,
Envy, and ignorance, to lift their state
Above a vulgar height. True happiness
Consists not in the multitude of friends,
But in their worth, and choice. Nor would I have
Virtue a popular regard pursue:
Let them be good that love me, though but few.

Ben Jonson (c.1572–1637)

The Orange

At lunchtime I bought a huge orange –
The size of it made us all laugh.
I peeled it and shared it with Robert and Dave –
They got quarters and I had a half.

And that orange, it made me so happy,
As ordinary things often do
Just lately. The shopping. A walk in the park.
This is peace and contentment. It's new.

The rest of the day was quite easy.
I did all the jobs on my list
And enjoyed them and had some time over.
I love you. I'm glad I exist.

Wendy Cope (1945–)

19 MARCH

Friendship is No Plant of Hasty Growth

FROM *DE MONTFORT: A TRAGEDY,* ACT III, SCENE II

Friendship is no plant of hasty growth,
Tho' planted in esteem's deep-fixed soil, the slow
And gradual culture of kind intercourse
Must bring it to perfection.

Joanna Baillie (1762–1851)

The Owl and the Pussycat

The Owl and the Pussycat went to sea
  In a beautiful pea-green boat.
They took some honey, and plenty of money,
  Wrapped up in a five-pound note.
The Owl looked up to the stars above,
  And sang to a small guitar,
'O lovely Pussy! O Pussy, my love,
  What a beautiful Pussy you are,
      You are,
      You are!
What a beautiful Pussy you are!'

Pussy said to the Owl, 'You elegant fowl!
  How charmingly sweet you sing!
O let us be married! too long we have tarried:
  But what shall we do for a ring?'
They sailed away, for a year and a day,
  To the land where the Bong-tree grows,
And there in a wood a Piggy-wig stood,
With a ring at the end of his nose,
      His nose,
      His nose.
With a ring at the end of his nose.

'Dear Pig, are you willing to sell for one shilling
  Your ring?' Said the Piggy, 'I will.'
So they took it away and were married next day
  By the Turkey who lives on the hill.
They dined on mince, and slices of quince,
  Which they ate with a runcible spoon;
And hand in hand, on the edge of the sand
  They danced by the light of the moon,
      The moon,
      The moon,
They danced by the light of the moon.

Edward Lear (1812–1888)

Passages of the Poem, or Connected Therewith

LINES 78–92

If I had but a friend! Why, I have three
Even by my own confession; there may be
Some more, for what I know, for 'tis my mind
To call my friends all who are wise and kind, –
And these, Heaven knows, at best are very few;
But none can ever be more dear than you.
Why should they be? My muse has lost her wings,
Or like a dying swan who soars and sings,
I should describe you in heroic style,
But as it is, are you not void of guile?
A lovely soul, formed to be blessed and bless:
A well of sealed and secret happiness;
A lute which those whom Love has taught to play
Make music on to cheer the roughest day,
And enchant sadness till it sleeps? ...

Percy Bysshe Shelley (1792–1822)

Song

Now the Spring is waking,
  Very shy as yet,
Busy mending, making
  Grass and violet,
Frowsy Winter's over;
  See the budding lane!
Go and meet your lover;
  Spring is here again!

Every day is longer
  Than the day before;
Lambs are whiter, stronger,
  Birds sing more and more;
Woods are less than shady,
  Griefs are more than vain –
Go and kiss your lady;
  Spring is here again!

E. Nesbit (1858–1924)

23 MARCH

Pangur Bán

I and Pangur Bán my cat,
'Tis a like task we are at:
Hunting mice is his delight,
Hunting words I sit all night.

Better far than praise of men
'Tis to sit with book and pen;
Pangur bears me no ill-will,
He too plies his simple skill.

'Tis a merry task to see
At our tasks how glad are we,
When at home we sit and find
Entertainment to our mind.

Oftentimes a mouse will stray
In the hero Pangur's way;
Oftentimes my keen thought set
Takes a meaning in its net.

'Gainst the wall he sets his eye
Full and fierce and sharp and sly;
'Gainst the wall of knowledge I
All my little wisdom try.

When a mouse darts from its den,
O how glad is Pangur then!
O what gladness do I prove
When I solve the doubts I love!

So in peace our task we ply,
Pangur Bán, my cat, and I;
In our arts we find our bliss,
I have mine and he has his.

Practice every day has made
Pangur perfect in his trade;
I get wisdom day and night
Turning darkness into light.

Written by a student of the monastery of Corinthia on a copy of St Paul's *Epistles*, in the eighth century, translated from the Gaelic by Robin Flower (1881–1946)

Lines

WRITTEN AT A SMALL DISTANCE FROM MY HOUSE, AND SENT BY MY LITTLE BOY TO THE PERSON TO WHOM THEY ARE ADDRESSED

FROM *LYRICAL BALLADS*

It is the first mild day of March:
Each minute sweeter than before
The red-breast sings from the tall larch
That stands beside our door.

There is a blessing in the air,
Which seems a sense of joy to yield
To the bare trees, and mountains bare,
And grass in the green field.

My Sister! ('tis a wish of mine)
Now that our morning meal is done,
Make haste, your morning task resign;
Come forth and feel the sun.

Edward will come with you; and pray,
Put on with speed your woodland dress,
And bring no book, for this one day
We'll give to idleness.

No joyless forms shall regulate
Our living Calendar:
We from to-day, my friend, will date
The opening of the year.

Love, now a universal birth,
From heart to heart is stealing,
From earth to man, from man to earth,
– It is the hour of feeling.

One moment now may give us more
Than fifty years of reason:
Our minds shall drink at every pore
The spirit of the season.

Some silent laws our hearts may make,
Which they shall long obey;
We for the year to come may take
Our temper from to-day.

And from the blessed power that rolls
About, below, above,
We'll frame the measure of our souls,
They shall be tuned to love.

Then come, my sister! come, I pray,
With speed put on your woodland dress;
And bring no book; for this one day
We'll give to idleness.

William Wordsworth (1770–1850)

An Ode for Ben Jonson

Ah *Ben*!
Say how, or when
Shall we thy Guests
Meet at those *Lyrick* Feasts,
Made at the *Sun*,
The Dog, the triple *Tunne*?
Where we such clusters had,
As made us nobly wild, not mad;
And yet each Verse of thine
Out-did the meate, out-did the frolick wine.

My *Ben*
Or come agen,
Or send to us,
Thy wits great over-plus;
But teach us yet
Wisely to husband it;
Lest we that Tallent spend:
And having once brought to an end
That precious stock; the store
Of such a wit the world sho'd have no more.

Robert Herrick (1591–1674)

Tea With Laura

laura raises the empty teacup to my lips
—the ritual oft-rehearsed—then smiles.
(*'would you like some cake?'* she says.)

the nursery carpet strewn with crumbs, teddy bears
—silent faces much like mine—and dolls.
(*'you're my favourite,'* she says.)

she combs my hair most carefully, three times a day
—i try not to blink, of course—at least.
(*'but, your shoelaces!'* she says.)

*

she finds me in the loft between two crates of books
—my eyes now coated with dust—and clothes.
(*'oh. look what I've got,'* she says.)

i'm caught between two hands: the fingers with red nails
—gripping tightly, urgently—quite chipped.
(*'i'd not forgotten,'* she says.)

Joel Knight (1975–)

Rose-cheekt Lawra

FROM *OBSERVATIONS IN THE ART OF ENGLISH POESIE*

Rose-cheekt *Lawra*, come,
Sing thou smoothly with thy beawties
Silent musick, either other
Sweetely gracing.
Lovely formes do flowe
From concent divinely framed;
Heav'n is musick, and thy beawties
Birth is heavenly.
These dull notes we sing
Discords neede for helps to grace them;
Only beawty purely loving
Knowes no discord,
But still mooves delight,
Like cleare springs renu'd by flowing,
Ever perfect, ever in themselves eternall.

Thomas Campion (1567–1620)

Magdalene Walks

The little white clouds are racing over the sky,
And the fields are strewn with the gold of the flower of March,
The daffodil breaks under foot, and the tasselled larch
Sways and swings as the thrush goes hurrying by.

A delicate odour is borne on the wings of the morning breeze,
The odour of deep wet grass, and of brown new-furrowed earth,
The birds are singing for joy of the Spring's glad birth,
Hopping from branch to branch on the rocking trees.

All the woods are alive with the murmur and sound of Spring,
And the rosebud breaks into pink on the climbing briar,
And the crocus-bed is a quivering moon of fire
Girdled round with the belt of an amethyst ring.

And the plane to the pine-tree is whispering some tale of love
Till it rustles with laughter and tosses its mantle of green,
And the gloom of the wych-elm's hollow is lit with the iris sheen
Of the burnished rainbow throat and the silver breast of a dove.

See! the lark starts up from his bed in the meadow there,
Breaking the gossamer threads and the nets of dew,
And flashing a-down the river, a flame of blue!
The kingfisher flies like an arrow, and wounds the air.

Oscar Wilde (1854–1900)

Talk Not of Wasted Affection

FROM *EVANGELINE, A TALE OF ACADIE*, PART THE SECOND I

Talk not of wasted affection, affection never was wasted;
If it enrich not the heart of another, its waters, returning
Back to their springs, like the rain, shall fill them full of refreshment;
That which the fountain sends forth returns again to the fountain.
Patience; accomplish thy labour; accomplish thy work of affection!
Sorrow and silence are strong, and patient endurance is godlike.
Therefore accomplish thy labour of love, till the heart is made godlike,
Purified, strengthened, perfected, and rendered more worthy of heaven!

Henry Wadsworth Longfellow (1807–1882)

The Praise of a True Frende

Who so that wisely weyes the profite and the price,
Of thinges wherin delight by worth is wont to rise.
Shall finde no jewell is so rich ne yet so rare,
That with the frendly hart in value may compare.
  What other wealth to man by fortune may befall,
But fortunes changed chere may reve a man of all.
A frend no wracke of wealth, no cruell cause of wo,
Can force his frendly faith unfrendly to forgo.
  If fortune frendly fawne, and lend thee welthy store,
Thy frendes conjoyned joy doth make thy joy the more
If frowardly she frown and drive thee to distresse,
His ayde releves thy ruthe, and makes thy sorrowe lesse.
  Thus fortunes pleasant frutes by frendes encreased be,
The bitter sharp and sowre by frendes alayde to thee.
That when thou doest rejoyce, then doubled is thy joy,
And eke in cause of care, the lesse is thy anoy.
  Aloft if thou do live, as one appointed here,
A stately part on stage of worldly state to bere:
Thy frende as only free from fraud will thee advise,
To rest within the rule of mean as do the wise.
  He seeketh to forsee the peril of thy fall.
He findeth out thy faultes and warnes thee of them all.
Thee, not thy luck he loves, what ever be thy case,
He is thy faithfull frend and thee he doth embrace.
  If churlish cheare of chance have thrown thee into thrall,
And that thy nede aske ayde for to releve thy fall:
In him thou secret trust assured art to have,
And succour not to seke, before that thou can crave.

Thus is thy frende to thee the comfort of thy paine,
The stayer of thy state, the doubler of thy gaine.
In wealth and wo thy frend, an other self to thee,
Such man to man a God, the proverb sayth to be.

As welth will bring thee frendes in louring wo to prove,
So wo shall yeld thee frendes in laughing wealth to love.
With wisdome chuse thy frende, with vertue him retaine:
Let vertue be the ground, so shall it not be vaine.

Anon

Early Friendship

The half-seen memories of childish days,
  When pains and pleasures lightly came, and went;
  The sympathies of boyhood rashly spent
In fearful wanderings through forbidden ways;
The vague, but manly, wish to tread the maze
  Of life to noble ends: whereon intent,
  Asking to know for what man here is sent,
The bravest heart must often pause, and gaze –
The firm resolve to seek the chosen end
Of manhood's judgement, cautious and mature:
  With strength no selfish purpose can secure; –
My happy lot is this, that all attend
  That friendship which came first, and which shall
    last endure.

Aubrey Thomas de Vere (1814–1902)

APRIL

The Spring is for Joy

Two Pewits

Under the after-sunset sky
Two pewits sport and cry,
More white than is the moon on high
Riding the dark surge silently;
More black than earth. Their cry
Is the one sound under the sky.
They alone move, now low, now high,
And merrily they cry
To the mischievous Spring sky,
Plunging earthward, tossing high,
Over the ghost who wonders why
So merrily they cry and fly,
Nor choose 'twixt earth and sky,
While the moon's quarter silently
Rides, and earth rests as silently.

Edward Thomas (1878–1917)

My Comforter

The world had all gone wrong that day
  And tired and in despair,
Discouraged with the ways of life,
  I sank into my chair.

A soft caress fell on my cheek,
  My hands were thrust apart.
And two big sympathizing eyes
  Gazed down into my heart.

I had a friend; what cared I now
  For fifty worlds? I knew
  One heart was anxious when I grieved –
My dog's heart, loyal, true.

'God bless him,' breathed I soft and low,
  And hugged him close and tight.
One lingering lick upon my ear
  And we were happy – quite.

Anon

Song

The Lark's in the sky love
The flower's on the lea
The whitethorn's in bloom love
To please thee and me
'Neath its shade we can rest love
And sit on the hill
And as last we met love
Enjoy the spring still

The spring is for lovers
The spring is for joy
O'er the moor where the plovers
Wir hover and cry
We'll seek the white hawthorn love
And sit on the hill
In the sweet sunny morn love
And be lovers still

Where the partridge is craiking
From morning to e'en
In the wheatlands awaking
That sprouts young and green
Where the brook dribbles past love
Down the willowy glen
And as we met last love
Be lovers again

The lark's in the grass love
Abuilding her nest
And the brook runs like glass love
'Neath the carrion crow's nest
There the wild woodbines twine love
And till the day's gone
Sun sets and stars shine love
I'll call thee my own

John Clare (1793–1864)

The Cherry Trees

Out of the dusk of distant woods
All round the April skies
Blossom-white, the cherry trees
Like lovely apparitions rise,

Like spirits strange to this ill world,
White strangers from a world apart,
Like silent promises of peace,
Like hope that blossoms in the heart.

Laurence Binyon (1869–1943)

A Legacy

Friend of my many years!
When the great silence falls, at last, on me,
Let me not leave, to pain and sadden thee,
A memory of tears.

But pleasant thoughts alone
Of one who was thy friendship's honored guest
And drank the wine of consolation pressed
From sorrows of thy own.

I leave with thee a sense
Of hands upheld and trials rendered less –
The unselfish joy which is to helpfulness
Its own great recompense;

The knowledge that from thine,
As from the garments of the Master, stole
Calmness and strength, the virtue which makes whole
And heals without a sign;

Yea more, the assurance strong
That love, which fails of perfect utterance here,
Lives on to fill the heavenly atmosphere
With its immortal song.

John Greenleaf Whittier (1807–1892)

On a Certain Lady at Court

I know the thing that's most uncommon;
  (Envy, be silent, and attend!)
I know a reasonable Woman,
  Handsome and witty, yet a Friend.

Not warp'd by Passion, aw'd by Rumour,
  Not grave thro' Pride, or gay through Folly,
An equal Mixture of good Humour,
  And sensible soft Melancholy.

'Has she no Faults then (Envy says), Sir?'
  Yes she has one, I must aver;
When all the World conspires to praise her,
  The Woman's deaf, and does not hear.

Alexander Pope (1688–1744)

The Shepherd

FROM *SONGS OF INNOCENCE*

How sweet is the Shepherd's sweet lot!
From the morn to the evening he strays;
He shall follow his sheep all the day,
And his tongue shall be fillèd with praise.

For he hears the lamb's innocent call,
And he hears the ewe's tender reply;
He is watchful while they are in peace,
For they know when their Shepherd is nigh.

William Blake (1757–1827)

April Rise

If ever I saw blessing in the air
  I see it now in this still early day
Where lemon-green the vaporous morning drips
  Wet sunlight on the powder of my eye.

Blown bubble-film of blue, the sky wraps round
  Weeds of warm light whose every root and rod
Splutters with soapy green, and all the world
  Sweats with the bead of summer in its bud.

If ever I heard blessing it is there
  Where birds in trees that shoals and shadows are
Splash with their hidden wings and drops of sound
  Break on my ears their crests of throbbing air.

Pure in the haze the emerald sun dilates,
  The lips of sparrows milk the mossy stones,
While white as water by the lake a girl
  Swims her green hand among the gathered swans.

Now, as the almond burns its smoking wick,
  Dropping small flames to light the candled grass;
Now, as my low blood scales its second chance,
  If ever world were blessed, now it is.

Laurie Lee (1914–1997)

The Arrow and the Song

I shot an arrow into the air,
It fell to earth, I knew not where;
For, so swiftly it flew, the sight
Could not follow it in its flight.

I breathed a song into the air,
It fell to earth, I knew not where;
For who has sight so keen and strong,
That it can follow the flight of song?

Long, long afterward, in an oak
I found the arrow, still unbroke;
And the song, from beginning to end,
I found again in the heart of a friend.

Henry Wadsworth Longfellow (1807–1882)

10 APRIL

Two is Better Than One

ECCLESIASTES 4:9–12

Two is better than one,
because they have a good reward for their labour.

For if they fall, the one will lift up his fellow,
but woe to him that is alone when he falleth:
for he hath not another to help him up.

Again, if two lie together,
then they have heat:
but how can one be warm alone?

And if one prevail against him,
two shall withstand him:
and a threefold cord is not quickly broken.

The King James Bible

I Heard a Linnet Courting

I heard a linnet courting
  His lady in the spring:
His mates were idly sporting,
  Nor stayed to hear him sing
    His song of love. –
I fear my speech distorting
    His tender love.

The phrases of his pleading
  Were full of young delight;
And she that gave him heeding
  Interpreted aright
    His gay, sweet notes, –
So sadly marred in the reading, –
    His tender notes.

And when he ceased, the hearer
  Awaited the refrain,
Till swiftly perching nearer
  He sang his song again,
    His pretty song: –
Would that my verses spake clearer
    His tender song!

Ye happy, airy creatures!
  That in the merry spring
Think not of what misfeatures
  Or cares the year may bring;
    But unto love
Resign your simple natures,
    To tender love.

Robert Bridges (1844–1930)

To Flush, My Dog

VERSES 1–9

Loving friend, the gift of one,
Who, her own true faith, hath run,
Through thy lower nature;
Be my benediction said
With my hand upon thy head,
Gentle fellow-creature!

Like a lady's ringlets brown,
Flow thy silken ears adown
Either side demurely,
Of thy silver-suited breast
Shining out from all the rest
Of thy body purely.

Darkly brown thy body is,
Till the sunshine, striking this,
Alchemize its dulness, –
When the sleek curls manifold
Flash all over into gold,
With a burnished fulness.

Underneath my stroking hand,
Startled eyes of hazel bland
Kindling, growing larger, –
Up thou leapest with a spring,
Full of prank and curvetting,
Leaping like a charger.

Leap! thy broad tail waves a light;
Leap! thy slender feet are bright,
Canopied in fringes.
Leap – those tasselled ears of thine
Flicker strangely, fair and fine,
Down their golden inches.

Yet, my pretty sportive friend,
Little is't to such an end
That I praise thy rareness!
Other dogs may be thy peers
Haply in these drooping ears,
And this glossy fairness.

But of thee it shall be said,
This dog watched beside a bed
Day and night unweary, –
Watched within a curtained room,
Where no sunbeam brake the gloom
Round the sick and dreary.

Roses, gathered for a vase,
In that chamber died apace,
Beam and breeze resigning –
This dog only, waited on,
Knowing that when light is gone,
Love remains for shining.

Other dogs in thymy dew
Tracked the hares and followed through
Sunny moor or meadow –
This dog only, crept and crept
Next a languid cheek that slept,
Sharing in the shadow.

Elizabeth Barrett Browning (1806–1861)

The Royal Mandate

FROM *SECOND EPISTLE TO JOHN LAPRAIK*

For thus the royal mandate ran,
When first the human race began;
'The social, friendly, honest man,
  Whate'er he be,
'Tis he fulfils great Nature's plan,
  And none but he.'

Robert Burns (1759–1796)

A Footprint in the Air

'Stay!' said the child. The bird said, 'No,
My wing has mended, I must go.
I shall come back to see you though,
One night, one day – '
            'How shall I know?'
'Look for my footprint in the snow.'

'The snow soon goes – oh, that's not fair!'
'Don't grieve. Don't grieve. I shall be there
In the bright season of the year,
One night, one day – '
            'But tell me, where?'
'Look for my footprint on the air.'

Naomi Lewis (1911–2009)

Mary's Lamb

Mary had a little lamb,
  Its fleece was white as snow;
And everywhere that Mary went
  The lamb was sure to go.

It followed her to school one day,
  That was against the rule;
It made the children laugh and play
  To see a lamb at school.

And so the teacher turned it out,
  But still it lingered near,
And waited patiently about
  Till Mary did appear.

Why does the lamb love Mary so?
  The eager children cry;
Why, Mary loves the lamb, you know,
  The teacher did reply.

Sarah Josepha Hale (1788–1879)

Fragment 10: Three Sorts of Friends

Though friendships differ endless *in degree*,
The *sorts*, methinks, may be reduced to three.
Ac quaintance many, and *Con* quaintance few;
But for *In* quaintance I know only two –
The friend I've mourned with, and the maid I woo!

Samuel Taylor Coleridge (1772–1834)

Request to His Love to Joyne Bountie with Beautie

The golden gift that Nature did thee geve
To fasten frends and feede them at thy wyll,
With fourme and favour, taught me to beleve.
How thow art made to shew her greatest skill.
Whose hidden vertues are not so unknowen,
But lively domes might gather at the furst
Where beauty so her perfect seede hath sowen,
Of other graces folow nedes there must.
Now certesse Garret, sins all this is true,
That from above thy giftes are thus elect:
Do not deface them than with fansies newe,
Nor change of mindes let not thy minde infect,
But mercy him thy frend, that doth thee serve,
Who seekes alway thine honour to preserve.

Henry Howard, Earl of Surrey (1517–1547)

On the Fifth Floor in "Montmartre"

on the fifth floor in montmartre
we made cigarettes from newspaper.
a ripple of smoke. the smell of candle
wax. horsemeat.

cobbles swam likes fishes' scales, from
the tale of our
fissured eyes, a glance of something
bigger, if not better.

café windows. sunlight soiled.
a cat's incessant peeping.

years later, in that downstairs room
off the old kent road, a quiet roaring in my
ears.
next door's radio, children yelling.
a walk to clear the head (as far as the pub
and back).

there, so very far from myth, the windows
rose
like prison walls.

best not to say
no more.

Joel Knight (1975–)

Of Friendship

Choose judiciously thy friends; for to discard them is
undesirable,
Yet it is better to drop thy friends, O my daughter, than to
drop thy 'H's.'
Dost thou know a wise woman? yea, wiser than the
children of light?
Hath she a position? and a title? and are her parties in the
Morning Post?
If thou dost, cleave unto her, and give up unto her thy body
and mind;
Think with her ideas, and distribute thy smiles at her
bidding:
So shalt thou become like unto her; and thy manners shall
be 'formed,'
And thy name shall be a Sesame, at which the doors of the
great shall fly open:
Thou shalt know every Peer, his arms, and the date of his
creation,
His pedigree and their intermarriages, and cousins to the
sixth remove:
Thou shalt kiss the hand of Royalty, and lo! in next
morning's papers,
Side by side with rumours of wars, and stories of
shipwrecks and sieges,
Shall appear thy name, and the minutiæ of thy head-dress
and petticoat,
For an enraptured public to muse upon over their
matutinal muffin.

Charles Stuart Calverley (1831–1884)

The Promise of a Constant Lover

As Lawrell leaves that cease not to be grene,
From parching sunne, nor yet from winters threte
As hardened oke that feareth no sworde so kene,
As flint for toole in twaine that will not frete.
As fast as rocke, or pillar surely set:
So fast am I to you, and ay have bene,
Assuredly whom I cannot forget,
For joy, for paine, for torment nor for tene.
For losse, for gaine, for frowning, nor for thret,
But ever one, yea both in calme and blast,
Your faithfull friende, and will be to my last.

Anon

You

You won't believe it. Perhaps you're too prosaic
  To fall for a poetic ache,
But your smile (when you smile), your eyes, your nose,
  Are far too beautiful for prose.

Don't credit this, my dear, if you don't want to.
  A poem, too, can be a pack of lies.
But if you don't, then I'll come back and haunt you.
  You'll find me hard to exorcise.

Douglas Dunn (1942–)

Song

Love lives beyond
The tomb, the earth, which fades like dew
I love the fond
The faithfull and the true

Love lives in sleep
The happiness of healthy dreams
Eve's dews may weep
But love delightfull seems

'Tis seen in flowers
And in the even's pearly dew
On earth's green hours
And in the heaven's eternal blue

'Tis heard in spring
When light and sunbeams warm and kind
On angel's wing
Bring love and music to the mind

And where is voice
So young so beautiful, and sweet
As nature's choice
Where spring and lovers meet

Love lives beyond
The tomb, the earth, the flowers, and dew.
I love the fond,
The faithfull, young and true.

John Clare (1793–1864)

Ode on the Installation of the Duke of Devonshire extract

LINES 97–105

Can we forget one friend,
Can we forget one face,
Which cheered us toward our end,
Which nerved us for our race?
Oh sad to toil, and yet forego
One presence which has made us know
To Godlike souls how deep our debt!
We would not, if we could, forget.

Charles Kingsley (1819–1875)

A Thunderstorm in Town

(A REMINISCENCE: 1893)

She wore a 'terra-cotta' dress,
And we stayed, because of the pelting storm,
Within the hansom's dry recess,
Though the horse had stopped; yea, motionless
  We sat on, snug and warm.

Then the downpour ceased, to my sharp sad pain,
And the glass that had screened our forms before
Flew up, and out she sprang to her door:
I should have kissed her if the rain
  Had lasted a minute more.

Thomas Hardy (1840–1928)

To My Excellent Lucasia, on Our Friendship

I did not live until this time
  Crowned my felicity,
When I could say without a crime,
  I am not thine, but thee.

This carcass breathed, and walked, and slept,
  So that the world believed
There was a soul the motions kept;
  But they were all deceived.

For as a watch by art is wound
  To motion, such was mine:
But never had Orinda found
  A soul till she found thine;

Which now inspires, cures and supplies,
  And guides my darkened breast:
For thou art all that I can prize,
  My joy, my life, my rest.

No bridegroom's nor crown-conqueror's mirth
  To mine compared can be:
They have but pieces of the earth,
  I've all the world in thee.

Then let our flames still light and shine,
  And no false fear control,
As innocent as our design,
  Immortal as our soul.

Katherine Philips (1632–1664)

Green

The dawn was apple-green,
  The sky was green wine held up in the sun,
The moon was a golden petal between.

She opened her eyes, and green
  They shone, clear like flowers undone
For the first time, now for the first time seen.

D. H. Lawrence (1885–1930)

The Bird a Nest

FROM *PROVERBS OF HELL* FROM *THE MARRIAGE OF HEAVEN AND HELL*

The bird a nest, the spider a web, man friendship.

William Blake (1757–1827)

A Bed of Forget-me-nots

Is love so prone to change and rot
We are fain to rear forget-me-not
By measure in a garden plot? –

I love its growth at large and free
By untrod path and unlopped tree,
Or nodding by the unpruned hedge,
Or on the water's dangerous edge
Where flags and meadowsweet blow rank
With rushes on the quaking bank.

Love is not taught in learning's school,
Love is not parcelled out by rule;
Hath curb or call an answer got? –
So free must be forget-me-not.
Give me the flame no dampness dulls,
The passion of the instinctive pulse,
Love steadfast as a fixèd star,
Tender as doves with nestlings are,
More large than time, more strong than death:
This all creation travails of –
She groans not for a passing breath –
This is forget-me-not and love.

Christina Rossetti (1830–1894)

These I Can Promise

I cannot promise you a life of sunshine;
I cannot promise riches, wealth, or gold;
I cannot promise you an easy pathway
That leads away from change or growing old.
But I can promise all my heart's devotion;
A smile to chase away your tears of sorrow;
A love that's ever true and ever growing;
A hand to hold in yours through each tomorrow.

Mark Twain (1835–1910)

The Lover

FROM *THE PARAGON*, BOOK I, CANTO III

He meets, by heavenly chance express,
  The destined maid; some hidden hand
Unveils to him that loveliness
  Which others cannot understand.
His merits in her presence grow,
  To match the promise in her eyes,
And round her happy footsteps blow
  The authentic air of Paradise.

Coventry Patmore (1823–1896)

MAY

Please Come Flying

The Daisy-button Tipp'd Wi' Dew

The daisy-button tipped wi' dew Green like the grass was sleeping
On every thing 'neath heaven blue In moonlight dew was weeping
In dark wood sung the Nightingale The moon shone round above me
My arms were clasped round Mary Gale My dearest do you love me?

Her head a woodbine wet wi' dew Held in the moonlight sleeping
And two in one together grew Wi' daisy-buds a weeping
O' Mary Gale sweet Mary Gale How round and bright above thee
The moon looks down on grassy vale My dearest can you love me?

How sweet the moonlight sleeps and still Firdale and hedge-row brere
The molewarp's mound and distant hill Is moonlight everywhere
The totter-grasses' pendalums Are still as night above me
The bees are gone and nothing hums My dearest do you love me?

The moonlight sleeps o'er wood and wall Sweet Mary while you're nigh me
Can any charm o' courtship fail And any joy pass by me?
The gossamer all wet wi' dew Hung on the brere above me
She leaned her cheek and said 'I do, And ever mean to love thee.'

John Clare (1793–1864)

Madonna of the Evening Flowers

All day long I have been working
Now I am tired.
I call: 'Where are you?'
But there is only the oak-tree rustling in the wind.
The house is very quiet,
The sun shines in on your books,
On your scissors and thimble just put down,
But you are not there.
Suddenly I am lonely:
Where are you?
I go about searching.

Then I see you,
Standing under a spire of pale blue larkspur,
With a basket of roses on your arm.
You are cool, like silver,
And you smile.
I think the Canterbury bells are playing little tunes,

You tell me that the peonies need spraying,
That the columbines have overrun all bounds,
That the pyrus japonica should be cut back and rounded.
You tell me these things.
But I look at you, heart of silver,
White heart-flame of polished silver,
Burning beneath the blue steeples of the larkspur,
And I long to kneel instantly at your feet,
While all about us peal the loud, sweet *Te Deums* of the
Canterbury bells.

Amy Lowell (1874–1925)

Remembrance

Friend of mine! whose lot was cast
With me in the distant past;
Where, like shadows flitting fast,

Fact and fancy, thought and theme,
Word and work, begin to seem
Like a half-remembered dream!

Touched by change have all things been,
Yet I think of thee as when
We had speech of lip and pen.

For the calm thy kindness lent
To a path of discontent,
Rough with trial and dissent;

Gentle words where such were few,
Softening blame where blame was true,
Praising where small praise was due;

For a waking dream made good,
For an ideal understood,
For thy Christian womanhood;

For thy marvellous gift to cull
From our common life and dull
Whatsoe'er is beautiful;

Thoughts and fancies, Hybla's bees
Dropping sweetness; true heart's-ease
Of congenial sympathies; –

Still for these I own my debt;
Memory, with her eyelids wet,
Fain would thank thee even yet!

And as one who scatters flowers
Where the Queen of May's sweet hours
Sits, o'ertwined with blossomed bowers,

In superfluous zeal bestowing
Gifts where gifts are overflowing,
So I pay the debt I'm owing.

To thy full thoughts, gay or sad,
Sunny-hued or sober clad,
Something of my own I add;

Well assured that thou wilt take
Even the offering which I make
Kindly for the giver's sake.

John Greenleaf Whittier (1807–1892)

The Noble Nature

It is not growing like a tree
In bulk, doth make Man better be;
Or standing long an oak, three hundred year,
To fall a log at last, dry, bald, and sere:
A lily of a day
Is fairer far in May,
Although it fall and die that night –
It was the plant and flower of Light.
In small proportions we just beauties see;
And in short measures life may perfect be.

Ben Jonson (c.1572–1637)

Spring

Nothing is so beautiful as Spring –
  When weeds, in wheels, shoot long and lovely and lush;
  Thrush's eggs look little low heavens, and thrush
Through the echoing timber does so rinse and wring
The ear, it strikes like lightnings to hear him sing;
  The glassy peartree leaves and blooms, they brush
  The descending blue; that blue is all in a rush
With richness; the racing lambs too have fair their fling.

What is all this juice and all this joy?
  A strain of the earth's sweet being in the beginning
In Eden garden. – Have, get, before it cloy,
  Before it cloud, Christ, lord, and sour with sinning,
Innocent mind and Mayday in girl and boy,
  Most, O maid's child, thy choice and worthy the winning.

Gerard Manley Hopkins (1844–1889)

The Friendly Cinnamon Bun

Shining in his stickiness and glistening with honey,
safe among his sisters and his brothers on a tray,
with raisin eyes that looked at me as I put down my money,
there smiled a friendly cinnamon bun, and this I heard
him say:

'It's a lovely, lovely morning, and the world's a lovely place;
I know it's going to be a lovely day.
I know we're going to be good friends; I like your
honest face;
Together we might go a long, long way.'

The baker's girl rang up the sale, 'I'll wrap your bun,'
said she.
'Oh no, you needn't bother,' I replied.
I smiled back at that cinnamon bun and ate him,
one two three,
and walked out with his friendliness inside.

Russell Hoban (1925–2011)

XXXI

FROM *MORE POEMS*

Because I liked you better
  Than suits a man to say,
It irked you, and I promised
  To throw the thought away.

To put the world between us
  We parted, stiff and dry;
'Good-bye,' said you, 'forget me.'
      'I will, no fear', said I.

If here, where clover whitens
  The dead man's knoll, you pass,
And no tall flower to meet you
  Starts in the trefoiled grass,

Halt by the headstone naming
  The heart no longer stirred,
And say the lad that loved you
  Was one that kept his word.

A. E. Housman (1859–1936)

XXIX

FROM *SONNETS FROM THE PORTUGUESE*

I think of thee! – my thoughts do twine & bud
About thee, as wild vines, about a tree,
Put out broad leaves, and soon there's nought to see
Except the straggling green which hides the wood.
Yet, O my palm-tree, be it understood
I will not have my thoughts instead of thee
Who art dearer, better! Rather instantly
Renew thy presence. As a strong tree should,
Rustle thy boughs, and set thy trunk all bare,
And let these bands of greenery which insphere thee
Drop heavily down, ... burst, shattered, everywhere!
Because, in this deep joy to see and hear thee
And breathe within thy shadow a new air,
I do not think of thee – I am too near thee.

Elizabeth Barrett Browning (1806–1861)

Invitation to Miss Marianne Moore

From Brooklyn, over the Brooklyn Bridge, on this fine morning,
  please come flying.
In a cloud of fiery pale chemicals,
  please come flying,
to the rapid rolling of thousands of small blue drums
descending out of the mackerel sky
over the glittering grandstand of harbor-water,
  please come flying.

Whistles, pennants and smoke are blowing. The ships
are signaling cordially with multitudes of flags
rising and falling like birds all over the harbor.
Enter: two rivers, gracefully bearing
countless little pellucid jellies
in cut-glass epergnes dragging with silver chains.
The flight is safe; the weather is all arranged.
The waves are running in verses this fine morning.
  Please come flying.

Come with the pointed toe of each black shoe
trailing a sapphire highlight,
with a black capeful of butterfly wings and bon-mots,
with heaven knows how many angels all riding
on the broad black brim of your hat,
  please come flying.

Bearing a musical inaudible abacus,
a slight censorious frown, and blue ribbons,
   please come flying.
Facts and skyscrapers glint in the tide; Manhattan
is all awash with morals this fine morning,
   so please come flying.

Mounting the sky with natural heroism,
above the accidents, above the malignant movies,
the taxicabs and injustices at large,
while horns are resounding in your beautiful ears
that simultaneously listen to
a soft uninvented music, fit for the musk deer,
   please come flying.

For whom the grim museums will behave
like courteous male bower-birds,
for whom the agreeable lions lie in wait
on the steps of the Public Library,
eager to rise and follow through the doors
up into the reading rooms,
   please come flying.
We can sit down and weep; we can go shopping,
or play at a game of constantly being wrong
with a priceless set of vocabularies,
or we can bravely deplore, but please
   please come flying.

With dynasties of negative constructions
darkening and dying around you,
with grammar that suddenly turns and shines
like flocks of sandpipers flying,
   please come flying.

Come like a light in the white mackerel sky,
come like a daytime comet
with a long unnebulous train of words,
from Brooklyn, over the Brooklyn Bridge, on this fine morning,
   please come flying.

Elizabeth Bishop (1911–1979)

Sonnet XVIII

Shall I compare thee to a summer's day?
Thou art more lovely and more temperate:
Rough winds do shake the darling buds of May,
And summer's lease hath all too short a date;
Sometime too hot the eye of heaven shines,
And often is his gold complexion dimmed;
And every fair from fair sometime declines,
By chance or nature's changing course untrimmed;
But thy eternal summer shall not fade,
Nor lose possession of that fair thou ow'st;
Nor shall death brag thou wander'st in his shade,
When in eternal lines to time thou grow'st:
  So long as men can breathe or eyes can see,
  So long lives this, and this gives life to thee.

William Shakespeare (1564–1616)

Compliments of a Friend

How many gifted pens have penned
That Mother is a boy's best friend!
How many more with like afflatus
Award the dog that honored status!
I hope my tongue in prune juice smothers
If I belittle dogs or mothers,
But gracious, how can I agree?
I know my own best friend is Me.
We share our joys and our aversions,
We're thicker than the Medes and Persians,
We blend like voices in a chorus,
The same things please, the same things bore us.
If I am broke, then Me needs money;
I make a joke, Me finds it funny.
I know what I like, Me knows what art is;
We hate the people at cocktail parties,
When I can stand the crowd no more,
Why, Me is halfway to the door.
I am a dodo; Me, an auk;
We grieve that pictures learned to talk;
For every sin that I produce
Kind Me can find some soft excuse,
And when I blow a final gasket,
Who but Me will share my casket?
Beside us, Pythias and Damon
We're just two unacquainted laymen.
Sneer not, for if you answer true,
Don't you feel that way about You?

Ogden Nash (1902–1971)

Sweet Idyl

FROM *THE PRINCESS*, PART VII

Come down, O maid, from yonder mountain height:
What pleasure lives in height (the shepherd sang)
In height and cold, the splendour of the hills?
But cease to move so near the Heavens, and cease
To glide a sunbeam by the blasted Pine,
To sit a star upon the sparkling spire;
And come, for Love is of the valley, come,
For Love is of the valley, come thou down
And find him; by the happy threshold, he,
Or hand in hand with Plenty in the maize,
Or red with spirted purple of the vats,
Or foxlike in the vine; nor cares to walk
With Death and Morning on the silver horns,
Nor wilt thou snare him in the white ravine,
Nor find him dropt upon the firths of ice,
That huddling slant in furrow-cloven falls
To roll the torrent out of dusky doors:
But follow; let the torrent dance thee down
To find him in the valley; let the wild
Lean-headed Eagles yelp alone, and leave
The monstrous ledges there to slope, and spill

Their thousand wreaths of dangling water-smoke,
That like a broken purpose waste in air:
So waste not thou; but come; for all the vales
Await thee; azure pillars of the hearth
Arise to thee; the children call, and I
Thy shepherd pipe, and sweet is every sound,
Sweeter thy voice, but every sound is sweet;
Myriads of rivulets hurrying thro' the lawn,
The moan of doves in immemorial elms,
And murmuring of innumerable bees.

Alfred, Lord Tennyson (1809–1892)

Relationships

Understanding must be on both sides,
Confidence with confidence, and every talk
Be like a long and needed walk
When flowers are picked, and almost – asides
Exchanged. Love is always like this
Even when there's no touch or kiss.

There are many kinds of relationships
But this is the best, as Plato said –
Even when it begins in a bed,
The gentle touching of hands and lips –
It is from such kindness friendship is made
Often, a thing not to be repaid

Since there is no price, no counting up
This and that, gift. Humility
Is the essential ability
Before the loved object. Oh, we can sip
Something that tastes almost divine
In such pure sharing – yours and mine.

Elizabeth Jennings (1926–2001)

Louisa

AFTER ACCOMPANYING HER ON A MOUNTAIN EXCURSION. WRITTEN AT TOWN-END, GRASMERE

I met Louisa in the shade,
And, having seen that lovely Maid,
Why should I fear to say
That, nymph-like, she is fleet and strong,
And down the rocks can leap along
Like rivulets in May?

She loves her fire, her cottage-home;
Yet o'er the moorland will she roam
In weather rough and bleak;
And, when against the wind she strains,
Oh! might I kiss the mountain rains
That sparkle on her cheek.

Take all that's mine 'beneath the moon,'
If I with her but half a noon
May sit beneath the walls
Of some old cave, or mossy nook,
When up she winds along the brook
To hunt the waterfalls.

William Wordsworth (1770–1850)

The Passionate Shepherd to His Love

Come live with me and be my love,
And we will all the pleasures prove,
That hills and valleys, dales and fields,
And all the craggy mountains yields.

There we will sit upon the rocks,
And see the shepherds feed their flocks,
By shallow rivers to whose falls
Melodious birds sing madrigals.

And I will make thee beds of roses
With a thousand fragrant posies,
A cap of flowers, and a kirtle,
Embroidered all with leaves of myrtle;

A gown made of the finest wool
Which from our pretty lambs we pull;
Fair lined slippers for the cold,
With buckles of the purest gold;

A belt of straw and ivy-buds,
With coral clasps and amber studs:
And if these pleasures may thee move,
Come live with me and be my love.

The shepherds' swains shall dance and sing
For thy delight each May morning:
If these delights thy mind may move,
Then live with me and be my love.

Christopher Marlowe (1564–1593)

Spring Longing

The South wind blows open the folds of my dress,
My feet leave wet tracks in the earth of my garden,
The willows along the canal sing
        with new leaves turned upon the wind.

    I walk along the tow-path
    Gazing at the level water.
    Should I see a ribbed edge
    Running upon its clearness,
    I should know that this was caused
    By the prow of the boat
    In which you are to return.

Amy Lowell (1874–1925)

The Unseen Playmate

When children are playing alone on the green,
In comes the playmate that never was seen.
When children are happy and lonely and good,
The Friend of the Children comes out of the wood.

Nobody heard him, and nobody saw,
His is a picture you never could draw,
But he's sure to be present, abroad or at home,
When children are happy and playing alone.

He lies in the laurels, he runs on the grass,
He sings when you tinkle the musical glass;
Whene'er you are happy and cannot tell why,
The Friend of the Children is sure to be by!

He loves to be little, he hates to be big,
'Tis he that inhabits the caves that you dig;
'Tis he when you play with your soldiers of tin
That sides with the Frenchmen and never can win.

'Tis he, when at night you go off to your bed,
Bids you go to sleep and not trouble your head;
For wherever they're lying, in cupboard or shelf,
'Tis he will take care of your playthings himself!

Robert Louis Stevenson (1850–1894)

A Spring Morning

Spring cometh in with all her hues and smells
In freshness breathing over hills and dells
O'er woods where May her gorgeous drapery flings
And meads washed fragrant by their laughing springs
Fresh as new-opened flowers untouched and free
From the bold rifling of the amorous bee
The happy time of singing birds is come
And love's lone pilgrimage now finds a home
Among the mossy oaks now coos the dove
And the hoarse crow finds softer notes for love
The foxes play around their dens and bark
In joy's excess mid woodland shadows dark
The flowers join lips below the leaves above
And every sound that meets the ear is love

John Clare (1793–1864)

The Echoing Green

FROM *SONGS OF INNOCENCE*

The Sun does arise,
And make happy the skies;
The merry bells ring
To welcome the Spring;
The skylark and thrush,
The birds of the bush,
Sing louder around
To the bells' cheerful sound;
While our sports shall be seen
On the Echoing Green.

Old John, with white hair,
Does laugh away care,
Sitting under the oak,
Among the old folk.
They laugh at our play,
And soon they all say:
'Such, such were the joys
When we all, girls and boys,
In our youth time were seen
On the Echoing Green.'

Till the little ones, weary,
No more can be merry:
The sun does descend,
And our sports have an end.
Round the laps of their mothers
Many sisters and brothers,
Like birds in their nest,
Are ready for rest,
And sport no more seen
On the darkening Green.

William Blake (1757–1827)

She Was a Phantom of Delight

WRITTEN AT TOWN-END, GRASMERE. THE GERM OF THIS POEM WAS FOUR LINES COMPOSED AS PART OF THE VERSES ON THE HIGHLAND GIRL. THOUGH BEGINNING IN THIS WAY, IT WAS WRITTEN FROM MY HEART, AS IS SUFFICIENTLY OBVIOUS.

She was a Phantom of delight
When first she gleamed upon my sight;
A lovely Apparition, sent
To be a moment's ornament;
Her eyes as stars of Twilight fair;
Like Twilight's, too, her dusky hair;
But all things else about her drawn
From May-time and the cheerful Dawn;
A dancing Shape, an Image gay,
To haunt, to startle, and way-lay.

I saw her upon nearer view,
A Spirit, yet a Woman too!
Her household motions light and free,
And steps of virgin-liberty;
A countenance in which did meet
Sweet records, promises as sweet;
A Creature not too bright or good
For human nature's daily food;
For transient sorrows, simple wiles,
Praise, blame, love, kisses, tears, and smiles.

And now I see with eye serene
The very pulse of the machine;
A Being breathing thoughtful breath,
A Traveller between life and death;
The reason firm, the temperate will,
Endurance, foresight, strength, and skill;
A perfect Woman, nobly planned,
To warn, to comfort, and command;
And yet a Spirit still, and bright
With something of angelic light.

William Wordsworth (1770–1850)

Silent Noon

THE HOUSE OF LIFE, 19

Your hands lie open in the long fresh grass, –
The finger-points look through like rosy blooms
Your eyes smile peace. The pasture gleams and glooms
'Neath billowing skies that scatter and amass.
All round our nest, far as the eye can pass,
Are golden kingcup fields with silver edge
Where the cow-parsley skirts the hawthorn-hedge.
'Tis visible silence, still as the hour-glass.

Deep in the sun-searched growths the dragon-fly
Hangs like a blue thread loosened from the sky: –

So this wing'd hour is dropt to us from above.
Oh! clasp we to our hearts, for deathless dower,
This close-companioned inarticulate hour
When twofold silence was the song of love.

Dante Gabriel Rossetti (1828–1882)

Friendship

Such love I cannot analyse;
It does not rest in lips or eyes,
Neither in kisses nor caress.
Partly, I know, it's gentleness

And understanding in one word
Or in brief letters. It's preserved
By trust and by respect and awe.
These are the words I'm feeling for.

Two people, yes, two lasting friends.
The giving comes, the taking ends
There is no measure for such things.
For this all Nature slows and sings.

Elizabeth Jennings (1926–2001)

A Temple to Friendship

'A Temple to Friendship;' said Laura, enchanted,
'I'll build in this garden, – the thought is divine!'
Her temple was built and she now only wanted
An image of Friendship to place on the shrine.
She flew to a sculptor, who set down before her
A Friendship, the fairest his art could invent;
But so cold and so dull, that the youthful adorer
Saw plainly this was not the idol she meant.

'Oh! never,' she cried, 'could I think of enshrining
'An image whose looks are so joyless and dim; –
'But yon little god, upon roses reclining,
'We'll make, if you please, Sir, a Friendship of him.'
So the bargain was struck; with the little god laden
She joyfully flew to her shrine in the grove:
'Farewell,' said the sculptor, 'you're not the first maiden
'Who came but for Friendship and took away Love.'

Thomas Moore (1779–1852)

24 MAY

Friendship and Single Life Against Love and Marriage

LINES 76–81

Love drowsy days and stormy nights
Makes, and breaks friendship, whose delights
Feed, but not glut our Appetites.

Well-chosen friendship, the most noble
Of Vertues, all our joys makes double,
And into halves divides our trouble.

Sir John Denham (1615–1669)

Rondeau

Jenny kissed me when we met,
  Jumping from the chair she sat in;
Time, you thief, who love to get
  Sweets into your list, put that in:
Say I'm weary, say I'm sad,
  Say that health and wealth have missed me,
Say I'm growing old, but add,
  Jenny kissed me.

Leigh Hunt (1784–1859)

An Old Story

Strange that I did not know him then.
  That friend of mine!
I did not even show him then
  One friendly sign;

But cursed him for the ways he had
  To make me see
My envy of the praise he had
  For praising me.

I would have rid the earth of him
  Once, in my pride! ...
I never knew the worth of him
  Until he died.

Edwin Arlington Robinson (1869–1935)

The Sun Has Burst the Sky

The sun has burst the sky
Because I love you
And the river its banks.

The sea laps the great rocks
Because I love you
And takes no heed of the moon dragging it away
And saying coldly 'Constancy is not for you'.

The blackbird fills the air
Because I love you
With spring and lawns and shadows falling on lawns.

The people walk in the street and laugh
I love you
And far down the river ships sound their hooters
Crazy with joy because I love you.

Jenny Joseph (1932–2018)

Friendship is a Partnership

FROM *THE NICOMACHEAN ETHICS*, BOOK IX, CHAPTER XII

For friendship is a partnership, and as a man is to himself, so is he to his friend; now in his own case the consciousness of his being is desirable, and so therefore is the consciousness of his friend's being, and the activity of this consciousness is produced when they live together, so that it is natural that they aim at this. And whatever existence means for each class of men, whatever it is for whose sake they value life, in that they wish to occupy themselves with their friends; and so some drink together, others dice together, others join in athletic exercises and hunting, or in the study of philosophy, each class spending their days together in whatever they love most in life; for since they wish to live with their friends, they do and share in those things which give them the sense of living together. Thus the friendship of bad men turns out an evil thing (for because of their instability they unite in bad pursuits, and besides they become evil by becoming like each other), while the friendship of good men is good, being augmented by their companionship; and they are thought to become better too by their activities and by improving each other; for from each other they take the mould of the characteristics they approve – whence the saying 'noble deeds from noble men'.

Aristotle (384–322BC)
Translated by Rev. D. P. Chase (1820–1902)

Good-Night

The skylarks are far behind that sang over the down;
I can hear no more those suburb nightingales;
Thrushes and blackbirds sing in the gardens of the town
In vain: the noise of man, beast, and machine prevails.

But the call of children in the unfamiliar streets
That echo with a familiar twilight echoing,
Sweet as the voice of nightingale or lark, completes
A magic of strange welcome, so that I seem a king

Among men, beast, machine, bird, child, and the ghost
That in the echo lives and with the echo dies.
The friendless town is friendly; homeless, I am not lost;
Though I know none of these doors, and meet but
strangers' eyes.

Never again, perhaps, after to-morrow, shall
I see these homely streets, these church windows alight,
Not a man or woman or child among them all:
But it is All Friends' Night, a traveller's good-night.

Edward Thomas (1878–1917)

An Epitaph

Like thee I once have stemm'd the sea of life,
  Like thee have languish'd after empty joys,
Like thee have labour'd in the stormy strife,
  Been grieved for trifles, and amused with toys.

Forget my frailties; thou art also frail:
  Forgive my lapses; for thyself may'st fall:
Nor read unmoved my artless tender tale –
  I was a friend, O man, to thee, to all.

James Beattie (1735–1803)

First Love

Yes, I know that you once were my lover,
But that sort of thing has an end,
And though love and its transports are over,
You know you can still be – my friend:
I was young, too, and foolish, remember;
(Did you ever hear John Hardy sing?) –
It was then, the fifteenth of November,
And this is the end of the spring!

You complain that you are not well-treated
By my suddenly altering so;
Can I help it? – you're very conceited,
If you think yourself equal to Joe.
Don't kneel at my feet, I implore you;
Don't write on the drawings you bring;
Don't ask me to say, 'I adore you,'
For, indeed, it is now no such thing.

I confess, when at Bognor we parted,
I swore that I worshipped you then –
That I was a maid broken-hearted,
And you the most charming of men.
I confess, when I read your first letter,
I blotted your name with a tear –
But, oh! I was young – knew no better,
Could I tell that I'd meet Hardy here?

How dull you are grown! how you worry,
Repeating my vows to be true –
If I said so, I told you a story,
For I love Hardy better than you!
Yes! my fond heart has fixed on another,
(I sigh so whenever he's gone,)
I shall always love you – as a brother,
But my heart is John Hardy's alone.

Caroline Norton (1808–1877)

JUNE

An Accord in All Things

The Best Thing in the World

What's the best thing in the world?
June-rose, by May-dew impearled;
Sweet south-wind, that means no rain;
Truth, not cruel to a friend;
Pleasure, not in haste to end;
Beauty, not self-decked and curled
Till its pride is over-plain;
Light, that never makes you wink;
Memory, that gives no pain;
Love, when, so, you're loved again.
What's the best thing in the world?
– Something out of it, I think.

Elizabeth Barrett Browning (1806–1861)

Meet Me in the Green Glen

Love meet me in the green glen
  Beside the tall elm-tree
Where the Sweet briar smells so sweet agen
  There come wi me
        Meet me in the green glen

Meet me at the sunset
  Down in the green glen
Where we've often met
  By hawthorn-tree and foxes den
        Meet me in the green glen

Meet me in the sheep pen
  Where the briars smell ae een
Meet me in the green glen
  Where white thorn shades are green
        Meet me in the green glen

Meet me in the green glen
  By sweetbriar bushes there
Meet me by your own sen
  Where the wild thyme blossoms fair
        Meet me in the green glen

Meet me by the sweetbriar
  By the mole hill swelling there
When the west glows like a fire
    Gods crimson bed is there
        Meet me in the green glen

John Clare (1793–1864)

The Youth Who Carried a Light

I saw him pass as the new day dawned,
  Murmuring some musical phrase;
Horses were drinking and floundering in the pond,
  And the tired stars thinned their gaze;
Yet these were not the spectacles at all that he conned,
  But an inner one, giving out rays.

Such was the thing in his eye, walking there,
  The very and visible thing,
A close light, displacing the gray of the morning air,
  And the tokens that the dark was taking wing;
And was it not the radiance of a purpose rare
  That might ripe to its accomplishing?

What became of that light? I wonder still its fate!
  Was it quenched ere its full apogee?
Did it struggle frail and frailer to a beam emaciate?
  Did it thrive till matured in verity?
Or did it travel on, to be a new young dreamer's freight,
  And thence on infinitely?

Thomas Hardy (1840–1928)

When On a Summer's Morn

When on a summer's morn I wake,
  And open my two eyes,
Out to the clear, born-singing rills
  My bird-like spirit flies,

To hear the Blackbird, Cuckoo, Thrush,
  Or any bird in song;
And common leaves that hum all day,
  Without a throat or tongue.

And when Time strikes the hour for sleep,
  Back in my room alone,
My heart has many a sweet bird's song –
  And one that's all my own.

W. H. Davies (1871–1940)

Duet

FROM *BECKET*, ACT II, SCENE I

1. Is it the wind of the dawn that I hear in the pine overhead?
2. No; but the voice of the deep as it hollows the cliffs of the land.
1. Is there a voice coming up with the voice of the deep from the strand,
One coming up with a song in the flush of the glimmering red?
2. Love that is born of the deep coming up with the sun from the sea.
1. Love that can shape or can shatter a life till the life shall have fled?
2. Nay, let us welcome him, Love that can lift up a life from the dead.
1. Keep him away from the lone little isle. Let us be, let us be.
2. Nay, let him make it his own, let him reign in it – he, it is he,
Love that is born of the deep coming up with the sun from the sea.

Alfred, Lord Tennyson (1809–1892)

Song

The summer down the garden walks
  Swept in her garments bright;
She touched the pale still lily stalks
  And crowned them with delight;
She breathed upon the rose's head
  And filled its heart with fire,
And with a golden carpet spread
  The path of my desire.

The larkspurs stood like sentinels
  To greet her as she came,
Soft rang the Canterbury bells
  The music of her name.
She passed across the happy land
  Where all dear dreams flower free;
She took my true love by the hand
  And led her out to me.

E. Nesbit (1858–1924)

Dover Beach

The sea is calm tonight.
The tide is full, the moon lies fair
Upon the straits; – on the French coast the light
Gleams and is gone; the cliffs of England stand,
Glimmering and vast, out in the tranquil bay.
Come to the window, sweet is the night air!
Only, from the ling line of spray
Where the sea meets the moon-blanch'd land,
Listen! you hear the grating roar
Of pebbles which the waves draw back, and fling,
At their return, up the high strand,
Begin, and cease, and then again begin,
With tremulous cadence slow, and bring
The eternal note of sadness in.

Sophocles long ago
Heard it on the Ægæan, and it brought
Into his mind the turbid ebb and flow
Of human misery; we
Find also in the sound a thought,
Hearing it by this distant northern sea.

The Sea of Faith
Was once, at the full, and round earth's shore
Lay like the folds of a bright girdle furl'd.
But now I only hear
Its melancholy, long, withdrawing roar,
Retreating, to the breath
Of the night-wind, down the vast edges drear
And naked shingles of this world.

Ah, love, let us be true
To one another! for the world, which seems
To lie before us like a land of dreams,
So various, so beautiful, so new,
Hath really neither joy, nor love, nor light,
Nor certitude, nor peace, nor help for pain;
And we are here as on a darkling plain
Swept with confused alarms of struggle and flight,
Where ignorant armies clash by night.

Matthew Arnold (1822–1888)

Consolation

Though he, that ever kind and true,
Kept stoutly step by step with you,
Your whole long, gusty lifetime through,
Be gone a while before,
Be now a moment gone before,
Yet, doubt not, soon the seasons shall restore
Your friend to you.

He has but turned the corner – still
He pushes on with right good will,
Through mire and marsh, by heugh and hill,
That self-same arduous way –
That self-same upland, hopeful way,
That you and he through many a doubtful day
Attempted still.

He is not dead, this friend – not dead,
But in the path we mortals tread
Got some few, trifling steps ahead
And nearer to the end;
So that you too, once past the bend,
Shall meet again, as face to face, this friend
You fancy dead.

Push gaily on, strong heart! The while
You travel forward mile by mile,
He loiters with a backward smile
Till you can overtake,
And strains his eyes to search his wake,
Or whistling, as he sees you through the brake,
Waits on a stile.

Robert Louis Stevenson (1850–1894)

Laughing Song

FROM *SONGS OF INNOCENCE*

When the green woods laugh with the voice of joy,
And the dimpling stream runs laughing by;
When the air does laugh with our merry wit,
And the green hill laughs with the noise of it;

When the meadows laugh with lively green,
And the grasshopper laughs in the merry scene;
When Mary and Susan and Emily
With their sweet round mouths sing 'Ha, Ha, He!'

When the painted birds laugh in the shade,
Where our table with cherries and nuts is spread,
Come live, and be merry, and join with me,
To sing the sweet chorus of 'Ha, Ha, He!'

William Blake (1757–1827)

Cherry Ripe

There is a Garden in her face,
Where Roses and white Lillies grow;
A heav'nly paradice is that place,
Wherein all pleasant fruits doe flow.
There Cherries grow, which none may buy,
Till Cherry ripe themselves doe cry.

Those Cherries fayrely doe enclose
Of Orient Pearle a double row,
Which when her lovely laughter showes,
They looke like Rose-buds fill'd with snow;
Yet them nor Peere nor Prince can buy,
Till Cherry ripe themselves doe cry.

Her Eyes like Angels watch them still;
Her Browes like bended bowes doe stand,
Threatning with piercing frownes to kill
All that attempt with eye or hand
Those sacred Cherries to come nigh,
Till Cherry ripe themselves doe cry.

Thomas Campion (1567–1620)

At the Mid Hour of Night

At the mid hour of night, when stars are weeping, I fly
To the lone vale we loved, when life shone warm in thine eye,
  And I think that if spirits can steal from the regions of air
  To revisit past scenes of delight, thou wilt come to me there,
And tell me our love is remember'd, even in the sky.

Then I sing the wild song it was once rapture to hear,
When our voices, commingling, breathed like one on the ear,
  And, as Echo far off through the vale my sad orison rolls,
  I think, oh my love! 'tis thy voice from the kingdom of souls,
Faintly answering still the notes that once were so dear.

Thomas Moore (1779–1852)

The Sunlight On the Garden

The sunlight on the garden
Hardens and grow cold,
We cannot cage the minute
Within its nets of gold,
When all is told
We cannot beg for pardon.

Our freedom as free lances
Advances towards its end;
The earth compels, upon it
Sonnets and birds descend;
And soon, my friend,
We shall have no time for dances.

The sky was good for flying
Defying the church bells
And every evil iron
Siren and what it tells:
The earth compels,
We are dying, Egypt, dying

And not expecting pardon,
Hardened in heart anew,
But glad to have sat under
Thunder and rain with you,
And grateful too
For sunlight on the garden.

Louis MacNeice (1907–1963)

Hearts-Ease

There is a flower I wish to wear,
But not until first worne by you …
Hearts-ease … of all Earth's flowers most rare;
Bring it; and bring enough for two.

Walter Savage Landor (1775–1864)

The Little Dancers

Lonely, save for a few faint stars, the sky
Dreams; and lonely, below, the little street
Into its gloom retires, secluded and shy.
Scarcely the dumb roar enters this soft retreat;
And all is dark, save where come flooding rays
From a tavern-window; there, to the brisk measure
Of an organ that down in the alley merrily plays,
Two children, all alone and no one by,
Holding their tattered frocks, thro' an airy maze
Of motion lightly threaded with nimble feet
Dance sedately; face to face they gaze,
Their eyes shining, grave with a perfect pleasure.

Laurence Binyon (1869–1943)

Love and Age

I played with you 'mid cowslips blowing,
When I was six and you were four;
When garlands weaving, flower-balls throwing,
Were pleasures soon to please no more.
Through groves and meads, o'er grass and heather,
With little playmates, to and fro,
We wandered hand in hand together;
But that was sixty years ago.

You grew a lovely roseate maiden,
And still our early love was strong;
Still with no care our days were laden,
They glided joyously along;
And I did love you, very dearly,
How dearly words want power to show;
I thought your heart was touched as nearly;
But that was fifty years ago.

Then other lovers came around you,
Your beauty grew from year to year,
And many a splendid circle found you
The centre of its glistening sphere.
I saw you then, first vows forsaking,
On rank and wealth your hand bestow;
Oh, then I thought my heart was breaking, –
But that was forty years ago.

And I lived on, to wed another:
No cause she gave me to repine;
And when I heard you were a mother,
I did not wish the children mine.
My own young flock, in fair progression,
Made up a pleasant Christmas row:
My joy in them was past expression; –
But that was thirty years ago.

You grew a matron plump and comely,
You dwelt in fashion's brightest blaze;
My earthly lot was far more homely;
But I too had my festal days.
No merrier eyes have ever glistened
Around the hearth-stone's wintry glow,
Than when my youngest child was christened: –
But that was twenty years ago.

Time passed. My eldest girl was married,
And now I am a grandsire grey;
One pet of four years old I've carried
Among the wild-flowered meads to play.
In our old fields of childish pleasure,
Where now as then, the cowslips blow,
She fills her basket's ample measure, –
And that is not ten years ago.

But though love's first impassioned blindness
Has passed away in colder light,
I still have thought of you with kindness,
And shall do, till our last good-night.
The ever-rolling silent hours
Will bring a time we shall not know,
When our young days of gathering flowers
Will be a hundred years ago.

Thomas Love Peacock (1785–1866)

Song

Go lovely Rose
Tell her that wastes her time and me,
That now she knows,
When I resemble her to thee
How sweet and fair she seems to be.

Tell her that's young,
And shuns to have her graces spy'd,
That hadst thou sprung
In deserts where no men abide,
Thou must have uncommended dy'd.

Small is the worth
Of beauty from the light retir'd;
Bid her come forth,
Suffer herself to be desir'd,
And not blush so to be admir'd.

Then die that she
The common fate of all things rare
May read in thee;
How small a part of time they share,
That are so wondrous sweet and fair.

Edmund Waller (1606–1687)

Joys and Griefs

FROM *ON FRIENDSHIP*

There is no man, that imparteth his joys to his friend, but he joyeth the more: and no man that imparteth his griefs to his friend, but he grieveth the less. So that it is in truth of operation upon a man's mind, of like virtue as the alchemysts use to attribute to their stone for man's body; that it worketh all contrary effects, but still to the good and benefit of nature. But yet without praying in aid of alchemysts, there is a manifest image of this in the ordinary course of nature. For in bodies, union strengtheneth and cherisheth any natural action; and on the other side weakeneth and dulleth any violent impression: and even so it is of minds.

Francis Bacon (1561–1626)

Hiawatha's Friends

FROM *THE SONG OF HIAWATHA*, VI

Two good friends had Hiawatha,
Singled out from all the others,
Bound to him in closest union,
And to whom he gave the right hand
Of his heart, in joy and sorrow;
Chibiabos, the musician,
And the very strong man, Kwasind.
    Straight between them ran the pathway,
Never grew the grass upon it;
Singing birds, that utter falsehoods,
Story-tellers, mischief-makers,
Found no eager ear to listen,
Could not breed ill-will between them,
For they kept each other's counsel,
Spake with naked hearts together,
Pondering much and much contriving
How the tribes of men might prosper.

Henry Wadsworth Longfellow (1807–1882)

A Flower Given to My Daughter

Frail the white rose, and frail are
Her hands that gave
Whose soul is sere and paler
Than time's wan wave.

Rose-frail and fair – yet frailest
A wonder wild
In gentle eyes thou veilest,
My blue-veined child.

James Joyce (1882–1941)

Love's Good-Morrow

Pack, clouds away! and welcome day!
With night we banish sorrow;
Sweet air, blow soft, mount larks aloft
To give my love good-morrow!
Wings from the wind to please her mind,
Notes from the lark I'll borrow;
Bird, prune thy wing, nightingale, sing,
To give my love good-morrow;
To give my love good-morrow;
Notes from them both I'll borrow.

Wake from thy nest, Robin Redbreast,
Sing birds in every furrow;
And from each hill, let music shrill
Give my fair love good-morrow!
Blackbird and thrush in every bush,
Stare, linnet, and cock-sparrow!
You pretty elves, amongst yourselves,
Sing my fair love good-morrow;
To give my love good-morrow,
Sing birds in every furrow.

Thomas Heywood (c.1575–1641)

To a Friend

I ask but one thing of you, only one,
That always you will be my dream of you;
That never shall I wake to find untrue
All this I have believed and rested on,
Forever vanished, like a vision gone
Out into the night. Alas, how few
There are who strike in us a chord we knew
Existed, but so seldom heard its tone
We tremble at the half-forgotten sound.
The world is full of rude awakenings
And heaven-born castles shattered to the ground,
Yet still our human longing vainly clings
To a belief in beauty through all wrongs.
O stay your hand, and leave my heart its songs!

Amy Lowell (1874–1925)

I'm Nobody

I'm Nobody! Who are you?
Are you – Nobody – Too?
Then there's a pair of us
Don't tell! They'd advertise – you know!

How dreary – to be – Somebody!
How public – like a frog –
To tell your name – the livelong June –
To an admiring Bog!

Emily Dickinson (1830–1886)

The Invitation

Let us go into the fields love and see the green tree
Let's go in the meadows and hear the wild bee
There's plenty of pleasure for you love and me
   In the mirths and the music of nature
We can stand in the path love and hear the birds sing
And see the woodpigeons snap loud on the wing
While you stand beside me a beautiful thing
   Health and beauty in every feature

We can stand by the brig-foot and see the bright things
On the sun-shining water that merrily springs
Like sparkles of fire in their mazes and rings
   While the insects are glancing and twitters
You see naught in shape but hear a deep song
That lasts through the sunshine the whole summer long
That pierces the ear as the heat gathers strong
   And the lake like a burning fire glitters

We can stand in the fields love and gaze o'er the corn
See the lark from her wing shake the dews of the morn
Through the dew-bearded woodbine the gale is just born
   And there we can wander my dearie
We can walk by the wood where the rabbits pop in
Where the bushes are few and the hedge gapped and thin
There's a wild-rosy bower and a place to rest in
   So we can walk in and rest when we're weary

The skylark, my love, from the barley is singing
The hare from her seat of wet clover is springing
The crow to its nest on the tall elm swinging
  Bears a mouthful of worms for its young
We'll down the green meadow and up the lone glen
And down the woodside far away from all men
And there we'll talk over our love tales again
  Where last year the nightingale sung

John Clare (1793–1864)

Will You Come?

Will you come?
Will you come?
Will you ride
So late
At my side?
O, will you come?

Will you come?
Will you come?
If the night
Has a moon,
Full and bright?
O, will you come?

Would you come?
Would you come
If the noon
Gave light,
Not the moon?
Beautiful, would you come?

Would you have come?
Would you have come
Without scorning,
Had it been
Still morning?
Beloved, would you have come?

If you come
Haste and come.
Owls have cried;
It grows dark
To ride.
Beloved, beautiful, come.

Edward Thomas (1878–1917)

The Power of Friendship

FROM *LAELIUS DE AMICITIA*, 20

Moreover, how great the power of friendship is may most clearly be recognized from the fact that, in comparison with the infinite ties uniting the human race and fashioned by Nature herself, this thing called friendship has been so narrowed that the bonds of affection always united two persons only, or, at most, a few.

For friendship is nothing else than an accord in all things, human and divine, conjoined with mutual goodwill and affection, and I am inclined to think that, with the exception of wisdom, no better thing has been given to man by the immortal gods. Some prefer riches, some good health, some power, some public honours, and many even prefer sensual pleasures. This last is the highest aim of brutes; the others are fleeting and unstable things and dependent less upon human foresight than upon the fickleness of fortune. Again, there are those who place the 'chief good' in virtue and that is really a noble view; but this very virtue is the parent and preserver of friendship and without virtue friendship cannot exist at all.

Marcus Tullius Cicero (106–43BC)

Translated by William Armistead Falconer (1869–1927)

26 JUNE

Love Will Find Out the Way

VERSE 1

Over the mountains
  And over the waves,
Under the fountains
  And under the graves;
Under floods which are the deepest,
  Which do Neptune obey,
Over rocks which are the steepest,
  Love will find out the way.

Anon

A Red, Red Rose

My luve is like a red, red rose
  That's newly sprung in June;
My luve is like the melodie
  That's sweetly play'd in tune.
As fair art thou, my bonie lass,
  So deep in luve am I,
And I will luve thee still, my dear,
  Till a' the seas gang dry.

Till a' the seas gang dry, my dear,
  And the rocks melt wi' the sun!
I will luve thee still, my dear,
  While the sands o' life shall run.
And fare-thee-weel, my only luve,
  And fare-thee-weel a while!
And I will come again, my luve,
  Tho' it were ten-thousand mile.

Robert Burns (1759–1796)

Paying Calls

I went by footpath and by stile
  Beyond where bustle ends,
Strayed here a mile and there a mile
  And called upon some friends.

On certain ones I had not seen
  For years past did I call,
And then on others who had been
  The oldest friends of all.

It was the time of midsummer
  When they had used to roam;
But now, though tempting was the air,
  I found them all at home.

I spoke to one and other of them
  By mound and stone and tree
Of things we had done ere days were dim,
  But they spoke not to me.

Thomas Hardy (1840–1928)

To a Friend Who Sent Me Some Roses

As late I rambled in the happy fields,
  What time the sky-lark shakes the tremulous dew
  From his lush clover covert; – when anew
Adventurous knights take up their dinted shields;
I saw the sweetest flower wild nature yields,
  A fresh-blown musk-rose; 'twas the first that threw
  Its sweets upon the summer: graceful it grew
As is the wand that queen Titania wields.
And, as I feasted on its fragrancy,
  I thought the garden-rose it far excell'd;
But when, O Wells! thy roses came to me,
  My sense with their deliciousness was spell'd:
Soft voices had they, that with tender plea
  Whisper'd of peace, and truth, and friendliness unquell'd.

John Keats (1795–1821)

Of Frendship

LINES 1–22

Of all the heavenly giftes, that mortall men commend,
What trusty treasure in the world can countervail a frend?
Our helth is soon decayd: goodes, casuall, light and vain:
Broke have we sene the force of powre, and honour suffer stain.
In bodies lust, man doth resemble but base brute:
True vertue gets, and keeps a frend, good guide of our pursute:
Whose hearty zeale with ours accords, in every case:
No terme of time, no space of place, no storme can it deface.
When fickle fortune failes, this knot endureth still:
Thy kin out of their kinde may swarve, when frends owe the good will.
What sweter solace shall befall, than one to finde,
Upon whose brest thou mayst repose the secretes of thy minde?
He wayleth at thy wo, his teares with thine be shed:
With thee doth he all joyes enjoy: so leef a life is led.
Behold thy frend, and of thy self the pattern see:
One soull, a wonder shall it seem, in bodies twain to bee.
In absence, present, rich in want, in sicknesse sound,
Yea after death alive, mayst thou by thy sure frend be found.
Eche house, eche towne, eche realm, by stedfast love doth stand:
While fowl debate breeds bitter bale in eche devided land.
O frendship, flowr of flowrs: O lively sprite of life,
O sacred bond of blissfull peace, the stalworth staunch of strife:

Nicholas Grimald (1519–1562)

JULY

Memories that Endure

Evening Schoolboys

Harken that happy shout – the school-house door
Is open thrown and out the younkers teem
Some run to leapfrog on the rushy moor
And others dabble in the shallow stream
Catching young fish and turning pebbles o'er
For mussel clams – Look in that mellow gleam
Where the retiring sun that rests the while
Streams through the broken hedge – How happy seem
Those schoolboy friendships leaning o'er the stile
Both reading in one book – anon a dream
Rich with new joys doth their young hearts beguile
And the book's pocketed most hastily
Ah happy boys well may ye turn and smile
When joys are yours that never cost a sigh.

John Clare (1793–1864)

Love for Love's Sake

I'll range around the shady bowers
And gather all the sweetest flowers;
I'll strip the garden and the grove
To make a garland for my love.

When in the sultry heat of day
My thirsty nymph does panting lay,
I'll hasten to the river's brink
And drain the floods, but she shall drink.

At night to rest her weary head
I'll make my love a grassy bed
And with green boughs I'll form a shade
That nothing may her rest invade.

And while dissolved in sleep she lies,
My self shall never close these eyes;
But gazing still with fond delight
I'll watch my charmer all the night.

And then as soon as cheerful day
Dispels the darksome shades away,
Forth to the forest I'll repair
To seek provision for my fair.

Thus will I spend the day and night,
Still mixing labour with delight,
Regarding nothing I endure
So I can ease for her procure.

But if the nymph whom thus I love
To her fond swain should faithless prove,
I'll seek some distant shore
And never think of woman more.

Henry Carey (1687–1743)

3 JULY

An Hour's Discourse

FROM *ON FRIENDSHIP*

Friendship maketh indeed a fair day in the affections, from storm and tempests; but it maketh daylight in the understanding, out of darkness and confusion of thoughts. Neither is this to be understood only of faithful counsel, which a man receiveth from his friend; but before you come to that, certain it is that whosoever hath his mind fraught with many thoughts, his wits and understanding do clarify and break up, in the communicating and discoursing with another; he tosseth his thoughts more easily; he marshalleth them more orderly, he seeth how they look when they are turned into words: finally, he waxeth wiser than himself; and that more by an hour's discourse, than by a day's meditation.

Francis Bacon (1561–1626)

Charita

FROM *THE COUNTESS OF PEMBROKE'S ARCADIA*

My true love hath my hart, and I have his,
By just exchange, one for the other giv'ne.
I holde his deare, and myne he cannot misse:
There never was a better bargain driv'ne.

His hart in me, keepes me and him in one,
My hart in him, his thoughtes and senses guides:
He loves my hart, for once it was his owne:
I cherish his, because in me it bides.

His hart his wound receaved from my sight:
My hart was wounded, with his wounded hart,
For as from me, on him his hurt did light,
So still me thought in me his hurt did smart:
Both equall hurt, in this change sought our blisse:
My true love hath my hart and I have his.

Sir Philip Sidney (1554–1586)

Test Match at Lords

Bailey Bowling, McLean cuts him late for one.
I walk from the Long Room into slanting sun.
Two ramrod ancients halt as Stratham starts his run.
Then, elbows linked, but straight as sailors
On a tilting deck, they move. One, square-shouldered as a tailor's
Model, leans over, whispering in the other's ear:
'Go easy. Steps here. This end bowling.'
Turning I watch Barnes guide Rhodes into fresher air,
As if to continue an innings, though Rhodes may only play by ear.

Alan Ross (1922–2001)

Ode

We are the music-makers,
And we are the dreamers of dreams,
Wandering by lone sea-breakers,
And sitting by desolate streams.
World-losers and world-forsakers,
Upon whom the pale moon gleams;
Yet we are the movers and shakers,
Of the world forever, it seems.

With wonderful deathless ditties
We build up the world's great cities,
And out of a fabulous story
We fashion an empire's glory:
One man with a dream, at pleasure,
Shall go forth and conquer a crown;
And three with a new song's measure
Can trample an empire down.

We, in the ages lying
In the buried past of the earth,
Built Nineveh with our sighing,
And Babel itself with our mirth;
And o'erthrew them with prophesying
To the old of the new world's worth;
For each age is a dream that is dying,
Or one that is coming to birth.

Arthur William Edgar O'Shaughnessy (1844–1881)

Among All Lovely Things My Love Had Been

Among all lovely things my Love had been;
Had noted well the stars, all flowers that grew
About her home; but she had never seen
A glow-worm, never one, and this I knew.

While riding near her home one stormy night
A single glow-worm did I chance to espy;
I gave a fervent welcome to the sight,
And from my horse I leapt; great joy had I.

Upon a leaf the glow-worm did I lay,
To bear it with me through the stormy night:
And, as before, it shone without dismay;
Albeit putting forth a fainter light.

When to the dwelling of my Love I came,
I went into the orchard quietly;
And left the glow-worm, blessing it by name,
Laid safely by itself, beneath a tree.

The whole next day, I hoped, and hoped with fear;
At night the glow-worm shone beneath the tree;
I led my Lucy to the spot, 'Look here,'
Oh! joy it was for her, and joy for me!

William Wordsworth (1770–1850)

Song

I hid my love when young while I
Couldn't bear the buzzing of a flye
I hid my love to my despite
Till I could not bear to look at light
I dare not gaze upon her face
But left her memory in each place
Where ere I saw a wild flower lye
I kissed and bade my love good bye

I met her in the greenest dells
Where dewdrops pearl the wood blue bells
The lost breeze kissed her bright blue eye
The Bee kissed and went singing bye
A sun beam found a passage there
A gold chain round her neck so fair
As secret as the wild bees song
She lay there all the summer long

I hid my love in field and town
Till e'en the breeze would knock me down
The Bees seemed singing ballads o'er
The flyes buzz turned a Lions roar
And even silence found a tongue
To haunt me all the summer long
The Riddle nature could not prove
Was nothing else but secret love

John Clare (1793–1864)

The Rolling English Road

Before the Roman came to Rye or out to Severn strode,
The rolling English drunkard made the rolling English road.
A reeling road, a rolling road, that rambles round the shire,
And after him the parson ran, the sexton and the squire;
A merry road, a mazy road, and such as we did tread
The night we went to Birmingham by way of Beachy Head.

I knew no harm of Bonaparte and plenty of the Squire,
And for to fight the Frenchman I did not much desire;
But I did bash their baggonets because they came arrayed
To straighten out the crooked road an English drunkard made,
Where you and I went down the lane with ale-mugs in our hands,
The night we went to Glastonbury by way of Goodwin Sands.

His sins they were forgiven him; or why do flowers run
Behind him; and the hedges all strengthening in the sun?
The wild thing went from left to right and knew not which was which,
But the wild rose was above him when they found him in the ditch.
God pardon us, nor harden us; we did not see so clear
The night we went to Bannockburn by way of Brighton Pier.

My friends, we will not go again or ape an ancient rage,
Or stretch the folly of our youth to be the shame of age,
But walk with clearer eyes and ears this path that
  wandereth,
And see undrugged in evening light the decent inn
  of death;
For there is good news yet to hear and fine things
  to be seen,
Before we go to Paradise by way of Kensal Green.

G. K. Chesterton (1874–1936)

Uncle an' Aunt

How happy uncle us'd to be
O' zummer time, when aunt an' he
O' Zunday evenens, eärm in eärm,
Did walk about their tiny farm,
While birds did zing an' gnats did zwarm,
Drough grass a'most above their knees,
An' roun' by hedges an' by trees
   Wi' leafy boughs a-swaÿen.

His hat wer broad, his cwoat wer brown,
Wi' two long flaps a-hangen down;
An' vrom his knee went down a blue
Knit stocken to his buckled shoe;
An' aunt did pull her gown-taïl drough
Her pocket-hole, to keep en neat,
As she mid walk, or teäke a seat
   By leafy boughs a-swaÿen.

An' vu'st they'd goo to zee their lots
O' pot-eärbs in the geärden plots;
An' he, i'-may-be, by the hatch,
Would zee aunt's vowls upon a patch
O' zeeds, an' vow if he could catch
Em wi' his gun, they shoudden vlee
Noo mwore into their roosten tree,
   Wi' leafy boughs a-swaÿen.

An' then vrom geärden they did pass
Drough orcha'd out to zee the grass,
An' if the apple-blooth, so white,
Mid be at all a-touch'd wi' blight;
An' uncle, happy at the zight,
Did guess what cider there mid be
In all the orcha'd, tree wi' tree,
  Wi' tutties all a-swaÿen.

An' then they stump'd along vrom there
A-vield, to zee the cows an' meäre;
An' she, when uncle come in zight,
Look'd up, an' prick'd her ears upright,
An' whicker'd out wi' all her might;
An' he, a-chucklen, went to zee
The cows below the sheädy tree,
  Wi' leafy boughs a-swaÿen.

An' last ov all, they went to know
How vast the grass in meäd did grow
An' then aunt zaid 'twer time to goo
In hwome, – a-holden up her shoe,
To show how wet he wer wi' dew.
An' zoo they toddled hwome to rest,
Lik' doves a-vlee-en to their nest
  In leafy boughs a-swaÿen.

William Barnes (1801–1886)

Ballad

It was not in the winter
  Our loving lot was cast!
It was the time of roses,
  We plucked them as we passed!

That churlish season never frowned
  On early lovers yet ! –
Oh, no – the world was newly crowned
  With flowers, when first we met.

'Twas twilight, and I bade you go,
  But still you held me fast; –
It was the time of roses, –
  We plucked them as we passed!

What else could peer thy glowing cheek
  That tears began to stud? –
And when I asked the like of Love,
  You snatched a damask bud, –

And oped it to the dainty core
  Still glowing to the last: –
It was the time of roses,
  We plucked them as we passed!

Thomas Hood (1799–1845)

A Walk By the Water

Let us walk where reeds are growing,
  By the alders in the mead;
Where the crystal streams are flowing,
  In whose waves the fishes feed.

There the golden carp is laving,
  With the trout, the perch, and bream;
Mark! their flexile fins are waving,
  As they glance along the stream.

Now they sink in deeper billows,
  Now upon the surface rise;
Or from under roots of willows,
  Dart to catch the water-flies.

Midst the reeds and pebbles hiding,
  See the minnow and the roach –
Or by water-lilies gliding,
  Shun with fear our near approach.

Do not dread us, timid fishes,
  We have neither net nor hook;
Wanderers we, whose only wishes
  Are to read in Nature's book.

Charlotte Smith (1749–1806)

To Daisies, Not to Shut So Soone

1. Shut not so soon; the dull-ey'd night
  Ha's not as yet begunne
To make a seisure on the light,
  Or to seale up the Sun.

2. No Marigolds yet closed are;
  No shadowes great appeare;
Nor doth the early Shepherds Starre
  Shine like a spangle here.

3. Stay but till my Julia close
  Her life-begetting eye;
And let the whole world then dispose
  It selfe to live or dye.

Robert Herrick (1591–1674)

Audley Court

'The Bull, the Fleece are cramm'd, and not a room
For love or money. Let us picnic there
At Audley Court.'
I spoke, while Audley feast
Humm'd like a hive all round the narrow quay,
To Francis, with a basket on his arm,
To Francis just alighted from the boat,
And breathing of the sea. 'With all my heart,'
Said Francis. Then we shoulder'd thro' the swarm,
And rounded by the stillness of the beach
To where the bay runs up its latest horn.
We left the dying ebb that faintly lipp'd
The flat red granite; so by many a sweep
Of meadow smooth from aftermath we reach'd
The griffin-guarded gates, and pass'd thro' all
The pillar'd dusk of sounding sycamores,
And cross'd the garden to the gardener's lodge,
With all its casements bedded, and its walls
And chimneys muffled in the leafy vine.
There, on a slope of orchard, Francis laid
A damask napkin wrought with horse and hound,
Brought out a dusky loaf that smelt of home,
And, half-cut-down, a pasty costly-made,
Where quail and pigeon, lark and leveret lay,
Like fossils of the rock, with golden yolks
Imbedded and injellied; last, with these,
A flask of cider from his father's vats,
Prime, which I knew; and so we sat and eat

And talk'd old matters over; who was dead,
Who married, who was like to be, and how
The races went, and who would rent the hall:
Then touch'd upon the game, how scarce it was
This season; glancing thence, discuss'd the farm,
The four-field system, and the price of grain;
And struck upon the corn-laws, where we split,
And came again together on the king
With heated faces; till he laugh'd aloud;
And, while the blackbird on the pippin hung
To hear him, clapt his hand in mine and sang –

'Oh! who would fight and march and countermarch,
Be shot for sixpence in a battle-field,
And shovell'd up into some bloody trench
Where no one knows? but let me live my life.

'Oh! who would cast and balance at a desk,
Perch'd like a crow upon a three-legg'd stool,
Till all his juice is dried, and all his joints
Are full of chalk? but let me live my life.

'Who'd serve the state? for if I carved my name
Upon the cliffs that guard my native land,
I might as well have traced it in the sands;
The sea wastes all: but let me live my life.

'Oh! who would love? I woo'd a woman once,
But she was sharper than an eastern wind,
And all my heart turn'd from her, as a thorn
Turns from the sea; but let me live my life.'

He sang his song, and I replied with mine:

I found it in a volume, all of songs,
Knock'd down to me, when old Sir Robert's pride,
His books – the more the pity, so I said –
Came to the hammer here in March – and this –
I set the words, and added names I knew.
  'Sleep, Ellen Aubrey, sleep, and dream of me:
Sleep, Ellen, folded in thy sister's arm,
And sleeping, haply dream her arm is mine.
  'Sleep, Ellen, folded in Emilia's arm;
Emilia, fairer than all else but thou,
For thou art fairer than all else that is.
  'Sleep, breathing health and peace upon her breast:
Sleep, breathing love and trust against her lip:
I go to-night: I come to-morrow morn.
  'I go, but I return: I would I were
The pilot of the darkness and the dream.
Sleep, Ellen Aubrey, love, and dream of me.'
  So sang we each to either, Francis Hale,
The farmer's son, who lived across the bay,
My friend; and I, that having wherewithal,
And in the fallow leisure of my life
A rolling stone of here and everywhere,
Did what I would; but ere the night we rose
And saunter'd home beneath a moon, that, just
In crescent, dimly rain'd about the leaf
Twilights of airy silver, till we reach'd
The limit of the hills; and as we sank
From rock to rock upon the glooming quay,

The town was hush'd beneath us: lower down
The bay was oily calm; the harbour-buoy,
Sole star of phosphorescence in the calm,
With one green sparkle ever and anon
Dipt by itself, and we were glad at heart.

Alfred, Lord Tennyson (1809–1892)

15 JULY

L'amitié, est L'amour Sans Ailes

VERSE 1

Why should my anxious breast repine,
Because my youth is fled?
Days of delight may still be mine;
Affection is not dead.
In tracing back the years of youth,
One firm record, one lasting truth
Celestial consolation brings;
Bear it, ye breezes, to the seat,
Where first my heart responsive beat, –
'Friendship is Love without his wings!'

George Gordon, Lord Byron (1788–1824)

16 JULY

Here's Health

Here's health to those that I love
Here's health to those that love me
Here's health to those that love those that I love
And those that love those that love me.

Anon

17 JULY

The Rainbow

Even the rainbow has a body
made of drizzling rain
and it is an architecture of glistening atoms
built up, built up
yet you can't lay your hand on it,
nay, nor even your mind.

D. H. Lawrence (1885–1930)

To a Friend

You entered my life in a casual way,
  And saw at a glance what I needed;
There came others who passed me or met me each day,
  But never a one of them heeded.
Perhaps you were thinking of other folks more,
  Or chance simply seem to decree it;
I know there were many such chances before,
  But the others – well, they didn't see it.

You said just the thing that I wished you would say,
  And you made me believe that you meant it;
I held up my head in the old gallant way,
  And resolved you should never repent it.
There are times when encouragement means such a lot,
  And a word is enough to convey it;
There were others who could have, as easy as not –
  But, just the same, they didn't say it.

There may have been someone who could have done more
  To help me along, though I doubt it;
What I needed was cheering, and always before
  They had let me plod onward without it.
You helped me to refashion the dream of my heart,
  And made me turn eagerly to it;
There were others who might have (I question that part) –
  But, after all, they didn't do it!

Grace Stricker Dawson (1891–?)

An Epitaph

His friends he loved. His direst earthly foes –
  Cats – I believe he did but feign to hate.
My hand will miss the insinuated nose,
  Mine eyes the tail that wagg'd contempt at Fate.

Sir William Watson (1858–1935)

To Electra

1. I dare not ask to kisse,
  I dare not beg a smile;
Lest having that, or this,
  I might grow proud the while.

No, no, the utmost share
  Of my desire, shall be
Onely to kisse that Aire,
  That lately kissed thee.

Robert Herrick (1591–1674)

Leisure

What is this life, if full of care,
We have no time to stand and stare.

No time to stand beneath the boughs
And stare as long as sheep or cows.

No time to see, when woods we pass,
Where squirrels hide their nuts in grass.

No time to see, in broad daylight,
Streams full of stars like skies at night.

No time to turn at Beauty's glance,
And watch her feet, how they can dance.

No time to wait till her mouth can
Enrich that smile her eyes began.

A poor life this, if full of care,
We have no time to stand and stare.

W. H. Davies (1871–1940)

The Faithful Friend

The green-house is my summer seat;
My shrubs displac'd from that retreat
  Enjoy'd the open air;
Two goldfinches, whose sprightly song
Had been their mutual solace long,
  Liv'd happy pris'ners there.

They sang, as blithe as finches sing,
That flutter loose on golden wing,
  And frolic where they list;
Strangers to liberty, 'tis true,
But that delight they never knew,
  And, therefore, never miss'd.

But nature works in ev'ry breast;
Instinct is never quite suppress'd;
  And Dick felt some desires,
Which, after many an effort vain,
Instructed him at length to gain
  A pass between his wires.

The open windows seem'd to invite
The freeman to a farewell flight;
  But Tom was still confin'd;
And Dick, although his way was clear,
Was much too gen'rous and sincere
  To leave his friend behind.

For, settling on his grated roof,
He chirp'd, and kiss'd him, giving proof
  That he desir'd no more;
Nor would his cage at last,
Till gently seiz'd I shut him fast,
  A pris'ner as before.

O ye, who never taste the joys
Of Friendship, satisfied with noise,
  Fandango, ball, and rout!
Blush when I tell you how a bird,
A prison, with a friend, preferr'd
  To liberty without.

William Cowper (1731–1800)

Side By Side

FRIEND AND FRIEND, VERSES 1–4

May we, then, never know each other?
Who love each other more, I dare
Affirm for both, than brother brother,
Ay! more, my friend, than they that are
The children of one mother.

A look – and lo, our natures meet!
A word – our minds make one reply!
A touch – our hearts have but one beat!
And, if we walk together – why
The same thought guides our feet

The self-same course! The flower that blows
A scent unguess'd in hedgerow green,
Slim spiders, where the water throws,
The starry-weeded stones between,
Strange light that flits and flows.

Were charged by some sweet spirit, sure,
(Love's minister, and ours!) to strike
Our sense with one same joy, allure
Our hearts, and bless us both alike
With memories that endure.

Edward Bulwer-Lytton / Owen Meredith (1831–1891)

Sonnet

When we were idlers with the loitering rills,
  The need of human love we little noted:
  Our love was nature; and the peace that floated
On the white mist, and dwelt upon the hills,
To sweet accord subdued our wayward wills:
  One soul was ours, one mind, one heart devoted,
  That, wisely doting, ask'd not why it doted,
And ours the unknown joy, which knowing kills.
But now I find how dear thou wert to me;
  That man is more than half of nature's treasure,
Of that fair beauty which no eye can see,
  Of that sweet music which no ear can measure;
  And now the streams may sing for others' pleasure,
The hills sleep on in their eternity.

Hartley Coleridge (1796–1849)

Friendship Between Ephelia and Ardelia

Eph. What Friendship is, Ardelia show.
Ard. 'Tis to love, as I love you.
Eph. This account, so short (tho' kind)
Suits not my inquiring mind.
Therefore farther now repeat:
What is Friendship when complete?
Ard. 'Tis to share all joy and grief;
'Tis to lend all due relief
From the tongue, the heart, the hand;
'Tis to mortgage house and land;
For a friend be sold a slave;
'Tis to die upon a grave,
If a friend therein do lie.
Eph. This indeed, tho' carried high,
This, tho' more than e'er was done
Underneath the rolling sun,
This has all been said before.
Can Ardelia say no more?
Ard. Words indeed no more can show:
But 'tis to love, as I love you.

Anne Finch, Countess of Winchelsea (1661–1720)

Thine Eyes Still Shined

Thine eyes still shined for me, though far
  I lonely roved the land or sea:
As I behold yon evening star,
  Which yet beholds not me.

This morn I climbed the misty hill
  And roamed the pastures through;
How danced thy form before my path
  Amidst the deep-eyed dew!

When the redbird spread his sable wing,
  And showed his side of flame;
When the rosebud ripened to the rose,
  In both I read thy name.

Ralph Waldo Emerson (1803–1882)

Ode

LINES 31–56

Words are easy, like the wind;
Faithful friends are hard to find;
Every man will be thy friend,
Whilst thou has wherewith to spend;
But, if store of coins be scant,
No man will supply thy want.
If that one be prodigal,
Bountiful, they will him call;
And with such-like flattering,
Pity but he were a king.
If he be addict to vice,
Quickly him they will entice.
If to women he be bent,
They have at commandement.
But if Fortune once do frown,
Then farewell his great renown;
They that fawned on him before
Use his company no more.
He, that is thy friend indeed,
He will help thee in thy need;
If thou sorrow, he will weep;
If thou wake, he cannot sleep;
Thus, of every grief, in heart,
He with thee doth bear a part.
These are certain signs to know
Faithful friend from flattering foe.

Richard Barnfield (1574–1627)

Us Two

Wherever I am, there's always Pooh,
There's always Pooh and Me.
Whatever I do, he wants to do,
'Where are you going to-day?' says Pooh:
'Well, that's very odd 'cos I was too.
Let's go together,' says Pooh, says he.
'Let's go together,' says Pooh.

'What's twice eleven?' I said to Pooh,
('Twice what?' said Pooh to Me.)
'I *think* it ought to be twenty-two.'
'Just what I think myself,' said Pooh.
'It wasn't an easy sum to do,
But that's what it is,' said Pooh, said he.
'That's what it is,' said Pooh.

'Let's look for dragons,' I said to Pooh.
'Yes, let's,' said Pooh to Me.
We crossed the river and found a few –
'Yes, those are dragons all right,' said Pooh.
'As soon as I saw their beaks I knew.
That's what they are,' said Pooh, said he.
'That's what they are,' said Pooh.

'Let's frighten the dragons,' I said to Pooh.
'That's right,' said Pooh to Me.
'*I'm* not afraid,' I said to Pooh,
And I held his paw and I shouted 'Shoo!
Silly old dragons!' – and off they flew.
'I wasn't afraid,' said Pooh, said he,
'I'm never afraid with you.'

So wherever I am, there's always Pooh,
There's always Pooh and Me.
'What would I do?' I said to Pooh,
'If it wasn't for you,' and Pooh said: 'True,
It isn't much fun for One, but Two,
Can stick together', says Pooh, says he.
'That's how it is,' says Pooh.

A. A. Milne (1882–1956)

Two Fusiliers

And have we done with War at last?
Well, we've been lucky devils both,
And there's no need of pledge or oath
To bind our lovely friendship fast,
By firmer stuff
Close bound enough.

By wire and wood and stake we're bound,
By Fricourt and by Festubert,
By whipping rain, by the sun's glare,
By all the misery and loud sound,
By a Spring day,
By Picard clay.

Show me the two so closely bound
As we, by the wet bond of blood,
By friendship blossoming from mud,
By Death: we faced him, and we found
Beauty in Death,
In dead men breath.

Robert Graves (1895–1985)

A Mile With Me

O who will walk a mile with me
  Along life's merry way?
A comrade blithe and full of glee,
Who dares to laugh out loud and free
And let his frolic fancy play,
Like a happy child, through the flowers gay
That fill the field and fringe the way
  Where he walks a mile with me.

And who will walk a mile with me
  Along life's weary way?
A friend whose heart has eyes to see
The stars shine out o'er the darkening lea,
And the quiet rest at the end o' the day –
A friend who knows, and dares to say,
The brave, sweet words that cheer the way
  Where he walks a mile with me.

With such a comrade, such a friend,
I fain would walk till journey's end,
Through summer sunshine, winter rain,
And then? – Farewell, we shall meet again!

Henry van Dyke (1852–1933)

To Thomas Moore

I

My boat is on the shore,
And my bark is on the sea;
But, before I go, Tom Moore,
Here's a double health to thee!

II

Here's a sigh to those who love me,
And a smile to those who hate;
And, whatever sky's above me,
Here's a heart for every fate.

III

Though the ocean roar around me,
Yet it still shall bear me on;
Though a desert should surround me,
It hath springs that may be won.

IV

Were't the last drop in the well,
As I gasp'd upon the brink,
Ere my fainting spirit fell,
'Tis to thee that I would drink.

V

With that water, as this wine,
The libation I would pour
Should be – peace with thine and mine,
And a health to thee, Tom Moore.

George Gordon, Lord Byron (1788–1824)

AUGUST

With Cheerful Greeting

1 AUGUST

Forsake Not an Old Friend

ECCLESIASTICUS 9:10

Forsake not an old friend,
for the new is not comparable to him:
a new friend is as new wine:
when it is old, thou shalt drink it with pleasure.

The King James Bible

Recuerdo

We were very tired, we were very merry –
We had gone back and forth all night on the ferry.
It was bare and bright, and smelled like a stable –
But we looked into a fire, we leaned across a table,
We lay on a hill-top underneath the moon;
And the whistles kept blowing, and the dawn came soon.

We were very tired, we were very merry –
We had gone back and forth all night on the ferry;
And you ate an apple, and I ate a pear,
From a dozen of each we had bought somewhere;
And the sky went wan, and the wind came cold,
And the sun rose dripping, a bucketful of gold.

We were very tired, we were very merry,
We had gone back and forth all night on the ferry.
We hailed, 'Good morrow, mother!' to a shawl-covered head,
And bought a morning paper, which neither of us read;
And she wept, 'God bless you!' for the apples and pears,
And we gave her all our money but our subway fares.

Edna St Vincent Millay (1892–1950)

Descending the Extreme South Mountain

PASSING THE HOUSE OF HU SSŬ, LOVER OF HILLS;
SPENDING THE NIGHT IN THE PREPARATION OF WINE

We come down the green-grey jade hill,
The mountain moon accompanies us home.
We turn and look back up the path:
Green, green, the sky; the horizontal, kingfisher-green line of the hills is fading.
Holding each other's hands, we reach the house in the fields.
Little boys thrown open the gate of thorn branches,
The quiet path winds among dark bamboos,
Creepers, bright with new green, brush our garments.
Our words are happy, rest is in them.
Of an excellent flavour, the wine! We scatter the dregs of it contentedly.
We sing songs for a long time; we chant them to the wind in the pine-trees.
By the time the songs are finished, the stars in Heaven's River are few.
I am tipsy. My friend is continuously merry.
In fact, we are so exhilarated that we both forget this complicated machine, the world.

Li Po (701–762)
Translated by Florence Ayscough (1878–1942)
and Amy Lowell (1874–1925)

Love Without Hope

Love without hope, as when the young bird-catcher
Swept off his tall hat to the Squire's own daughter,
So let the imprisoned larks escape and fly
Singing about her head, as she rode by.

Robert Graves (1895–1985)

5 AUGUST

Friendship

LINES 47–56

Friendship (like Heraldry) is hereby known,
Richest when plainest, bravest when alone;
Calme as a Virgin, and more innocent
Than sleeping Doves are, and as much content
As saints in visions; quiet as the night
But clear and open as the summer's light;
United more than spirits' facultys,
Higher in thoughts than are the Eagle's eys;
Free as first agents are true friends, and kind,
As but themselves I can no likeness find.

Katherine Philips (1632–1664)

To a Child

WRITTEN IN HER ALBUM

Small service is true service while it lasts;
Of humblest Friends, bright Creature! scorn not one:
The Daisy, by the shadow that it casts,
Protects the lingering dew-drop from the Sun.

William Wordsworth (1770–1850)

Jacke and Jone

Jacke and *Jone*, they think no ill,
But loving live, and merry still;
Doe their weeke dayes worke, and pray
Devotely on the holy day;
Skip and trip it on the greene,
And help to chuse the Summer Queene;
Lash out, at a Country Feast,
Their silver penny with the best.

Well can they judge of nappy Ale,
And tell at large a Winter tale;
Climbe up to the Apple loft,
And turne the Crabs till they be soft.
Tib is all the fathers joy,
And little *Tom* the mothers boy.
All their pleasure is content;
And care, to pay their yearely rent.

Jone can call by name her Cowes,
And decke her windows with greene boughs;
Shee can wreathes and tuttyes make,
And trimme with plums a Bridall Cake.
Jacke knows what brings gaine or losse,
And his long Flaile can stoutly tosse;
Make the hedges, which others breake,
And ever thinks what he doth speake.

Now, you Courtly Dames and Knights,
That study onely strange delights,
Thought you scorne the home-spun gray,
And revell in your rich array;
Though your tongues dissemble deepe,
And can your heads from danger keepe;
Yet, for all your pompe and traine,
Securer lives the silly Swaine.

Thomas Campion (1567–1620)

We Two Boys Together Clinging

We two boys together clinging,
One the other never leaving,
Up and down the roads going, North and South
excursions making,
Power enjoying, elbows stretching, fingers clutching,
Arm'd and fearless, eating, drinking, sleeping, loving,
No law less than ourselves owning, sailing, soldiering,
thieving, threatening,
Misers, menials, priests alarming, air breathing, water drinking,
on the turf or the sea-beach dancing,
Cities wrenching, ease scorning, statutes mocking,
feebleness chasing,
Fulfilling our foray.

Walt Whitman (1819–1892)

Fidelity

Fidelity and love are two different things, like a flower
 and a gem.
And love, like a flower, will fade, will change into
 something else
or it would not be flowery.

O flowers they fade because they are moving swiftly;
 a little torrent of life
leaps up to the summit of the stem, gleams, turns over
 round the bend
of the parabola of curved flight,
sinks, and is gone, like a comet curving into the invisible.

O flowers they are all the time travelling
like comets, and they come into our ken
for a day, for two days, and withdraw, slowly vanish again.

And we, we must take them on the wind, and let them go.
Embalmed flowers are not flowers, immortelles are
 not flowers;
flowers are just a motion, a swift motion, a
 coloured gesture;
that is their loveliness. And that is love.

But a gem is different. It lasts so much longer than we do
so much much much longer
that it seems to last forever.
Yet we know it is flowing away
as flowers are, and we are, only slower.
The wonderful slow flowing of the sapphire!

All flows, and every flow is related to every other flow.
Flowers and sapphires and us, diversely streaming.
In the old days, when sapphires were breathed upon
  and brought forth
during the wild orgasms of chaos
time was much slower, when the rocks came forth.
It took aeons to make a sapphire, aeons for it to pass away.

And a flower it takes a summer.

And man and woman are like the earth, that brings
  forth flowers
in summer, and love, but underneath is rock.
Older than flowers, older than ferns, older than
  foraminiferae
older than plasm altogether is the soul of a man
  underneath.

And when, throughout all the wild orgasms of love
slowly a gem forms, in the ancient, once-more-molten
  rocks
of two human hearts, two ancient rocks, a man's heart
  and a woman's,
that is the crystal of peace, the slow hard jewel of trust,
the sapphire of fidelity.
The gem of mutual peace emerging from the wild chaos
  of love.

D. H. Lawrence (1885–1930)

A Boy's Song

Where the pools are bright and deep,
Where the grey trout lies asleep,
Up the river and over the lea,
That's the way for Billy and me.

Where the blackbird sings the latest,
Where the hawthorn blooms the sweetest,
Where the nestlings chirp and flee,
That's the way for Billy and me.

Where the mowers mow the cleanest,
Where the hay lies thick and greenest,
There to track the homeward bee,
That's the way for Billy and me.

Where the hazel bank is steepest,
Where the shadow falls the deepest,
Where the clustering nuts fall free,
That's the way for Billy and me.

Why the boys should drive away
Little sweet maidens from the play,
Or love to banter and fight so well,
That's the thing I never could tell.

But this I know, I love to play
Through the meadow, among the hay;
Up the water and over the lea,
That's the way for Billy and me.

James Hogg (1770–1835)

Twilight Night

I

We met, hand to hand,
  We clasped hands close and fast,
As close as oak and ivy stand;
  But it is past:
  Come day, come night, day comes at last.

We loosed hand from hand,
  We parted face from face;
Each went his way to his own land.
  At his own pace,
  Each went to fill his separate place.

If we should meet one day,
  If both should not forget,
We shall clasp hands the accustomed way,
  As when we met
  So long ago, as I remember yet.

II

Where my heart is (wherever that may be)
  Might I but follow!
If you fly thither over heath and lea,
O honey-seeking bee,
  O careless swallow,
Bid some for whom I watch keep watch for me.

Alas! that we must dwell, my heart and I,
   So far asunder.
Hours wax to days, and days and days creep by;
I watch with wistful eye,
   I wait and wonder:
When will that day draw nigh – that hour draw nigh?

Not yesterday, and not, I think, to-day;
   Perhaps tomorrow.
Day after day 'tomorrow' thus I say:
I watched so yesterday
   In hope and sorrow,
Again today I watch the accustomed way.

Christina Rossetti (1830–1894)

All Here

It is not what we say or sing,
  That keeps our charm so long unbroken,
Though every lightest leaf we bring
  May touch the heart as friendship's token;
Not what we sing or what we say
  Can make us dearer to each other;
We love the singer and his lay,
  But love as well the silent brother.

Yet bring whate'er your garden grows,
  Thrice welcome to our smiles and praises;
Thanks for the myrtle and the rose,
  Thanks for the marigolds and daisies;
One flower erelong we all shall claim,
  Alas! unloved of Amaryllis –
Nature's last blossom-need I name
  The wreath of threescore's silver lilies?

How many, brothers, meet to-night
  Around our boyhood's covered embers?
Go read the treasured names aright
  The old triennial list remembers;
Though twenty wear the starry sign
  That tells a life has broke its tether,
The fifty-eight of 'twenty-nine –
  God bless the Boys! – are all together!

These come with joyous look and word,
With friendly grasp and cheerful greeting, –
Those smile unseen, and move unheard,
  The angel guests of every meeting;
They cast no shadow in the flame
  That flushes from the gilded lustre,
But count us – we are still the same;
  One earthly band, one heavenly cluster!

Love dies not when he bows his head
  To pass beyond the narrow portals, –
The light these glowing moments shed
  Wakes from their sleep our lost immortals;
They come as in their joyous prime,
  Before their morning days were numbered, –
Death stays the envious hand of Time, –
  The eyes have not grown dim that slumbered!

The paths that loving souls have trod
  Arch o'er the dust where worldlings grovel
High as the zenith o'er the sod, –
  The cross above the sexton's shovel!
We rise beyond the realms of day;
  They seem to stoop from spheres of glory
With us one happy hour to stray,
  While youth comes back in song and story.

Ah! ours is friendship true as steel
  That war has tried in edge and temper;
It writes upon its sacred seal
  The priest's *ubique – omnes – semper*!
It lends the sky a fairer sun
  That cheers our lives with rays as steady
As if our footsteps had begun
  To print the golden streets already!

The tangling years have clinched its knot
  Too fast for mortal strength to sunder;
The lightning bolts of noon are shot;
  No fear of evening's idle thunder!
Too late! too late! – no graceless hand
  Shall stretch its cords in vain endeavor
To rive the close encircling band
  That made and keeps us one forever!

So when upon the fated scroll
  The falling stars have all descended,
And, blotted from the breathing roll,
  Our little page of life is ended,
We ask but one memorial line
  Traced on thy tablet, Gracious Mother
'My children. Boys of '29.
  In pace. How they loved each other!'

Oliver Wendell Holmes (1809–1894)

First Shown

With you first shown to me,
With you first known to me,
My life-time loom'd, in hope, a length of joy:
Your voice so sweetly spoke,
Your mind so meetly spoke,
My hopes were all of bliss without alloy,
As I, for your abode, sought out, with pride,
This house with vines o'er-ranging all its side.

I thought of years to come,
All free of tears to come,
When I might call you mine, and mine alone,
With steps to fall for me,
And daycares all for me,
And hands for ever nigh to help my own;
And then thank'd Him who had not cast my time
Too early or too late for your sweet prime.

Then bright was dawn, o'er dew,
And day withdrawn, o'er dew,
And mid-day glow'd on flow'rs along the ledge,
And walls in sight, afar,
Were shining white, afar,
And brightly shone the stream beside the sedge.
But still, the fairest light of those clear days
Seem'd that which fell along your flow'ry ways.

William Barnes (1801–1886)

LIV

FROM *A SHROPSHIRE LAD*

With rue my heart is laden
  For golden friends I had,
For many a rose-lipt maiden
  And many a lightfoot lad.

By brooks too broad for leaping
  The lightfoot boys are laid;
The rose-lipt girls are sleeping
  In fields where roses fade.

A. E. Housman (1859–1936)

The Fountain

A CONVERSATION

We talked with open heart, and tongue
Affectionate and true,
A pair of friends, though I was young,
And Matthew seventy-two.

We lay beneath a spreading oak,
Beside a mossy seat;
And from the turf a fountain broke
And gurgled at our feet.

'Now Matthew!' said I, 'let us match
This water's pleasant tune
With some old border song, or catch
That suits a summer's noon;

'Or of the church-clock or the chimes
Sing here beneath the shade,
That half-mad thing of witty rhymes
Which you last April made!'

In silence Matthew lay, and eyed
The spring beneath the tree;
And thus the dear old Man replied,
The grey-haired man of glee:

‘No check, no stay, this Streamlet fears;
How merrily it goes!
’Twill murmur on a thousand years,
And flow as now it flows.

‘And here, on this delightful day,
I cannot choose but think
How oft, a vigorous man, I lay
Beside this fountain’s brink.

‘My eyes are dim with childish tears,
My heart is idly stirred,
For the same sound is in my ears
Which in those days I heard.

‘Thus fares it still in our decay:
And yet the wiser mind
Mourns less for what age takes away
Than what it leaves behind.

'The blackbird amid leafy trees,
The lark above the hill,
Let loose their carols when they please
Are quiet when they will.

'With Nature never do they wage
A foolish strife; they see
A happy youth, and their old age
Is beautiful and free:

'But we are pressed by heavy laws;
And often, glad no more,
We wear a face of joy, because
We have been glad of yore.

'If there be one who need bemoan
His kindred laid in earth,
The household hearts that were his own;
It is the man of mirth.

'My days, my Friend, are almost gone,
My life has been approved
And many love me; but by none
Am I enough beloved.'

'Now both himself and me he wrongs,
The man who thus complains;
I live and sing my idle songs
Upon these happy plains;

'And, Matthew, for thy children dead
I'll be a son to thee!'
At this he grasped my hand, and said,
'Alas! that cannot be.'

We rose up from the fountain-side;
And down the smooth descent
Of the green sheep-track did we glide;
And through the wood we went;

And, ere we came to Leonard's rock,
He sang those witty rhymes
About the crazy old church-clock,
And the bewildered chimes.

William Wordsworth (1770–1850)

The Meeting of the Waters

There is not in the wide world a valley so sweet
As that vale in whose bosom the bright waters meet;
Oh! the last rays of feeling and life must depart,
Ere the bloom of that valley shall fade from my heart.

Yet it was not that nature had shed o'er the scene
Her purest of crystal and brightest of green;
'Twas not her soft magic of streamlet or hill,
Oh! no, – it was something more exquisite still.

'Twas that friends, the belov'd of my bosom, were near,
Who made every dear scene of enchantment more dear,
And who felt how the best charms of nature improve,
When we see them reflected from looks that we love.

Sweet vale of Avoca! how calm could I rest
In thy bosom of shade, with the friends I love best,
Where the storms that we feel in this cold world should cease,
And our hearts, like thy waters, be mingled in peace.

Thomas Moore (1779–1852)

Beauty and Love

Beauty and love are all my dream;
  They change not with the changing day;
Love stays forever like a stream
  That flows but never flows away;

And beauty is the bright sun-bow
  That blossoms on the spray that showers
Where the loud water falls below,
  Making a wind among the flowers.

Andrew Young (1855–1971)

The Meeting of the Ships

'WE TAKE EACH OTHER BY THE HAND, AND WE EXCHANGE A FEW WORDS AND LOOKS OF KINDNESS, AND WE REJOICE TOGETHER FOR A FEW SHORT MOMENTS; AND THEN DAYS, MONTHS, YEARS INTERVENE, AND WE SEE AND KNOW NOTHING OF EACH OTHER.'

WASHINGTON IRVING

Two barks met on the deep mid-sea,
When calms had still'd the tide;
A few bright days of summer glee
There found them side by side.

And voices of the fair and brave
Rose mingling thence in mirth;
And sweetly floated o'er the wave
The melodies of earth.

Moonlight on that lone Indian main
Cloudless and lovely slept;
While dancing step, and festive strain
Each deck in triumph swept.

And hands were link'd, and answering eyes
With kindly meaning shone;
Oh! brief and passing sympathies,
Like leaves together blown.
A little while such joy was cast

Over the deep's repose,
Till the loud singing winds at last
Like trumpet music rose.

And proudly, freely on their way
The parting vessels bore;
In calm or storm, by rock or bay,
To meet – oh, never more!

Never to blend in victory's cheer,
To aid in hours of woe;
And thus bright spirits mingle here,
Such ties are formed below.

Felicia Hemans (1793–1835)

19 AUGUST

The Pleasures of Friendship

The pleasures of friendship are exquisite,
How pleasant to go to a friend on a visit!
I go to my friend, we walk on the grass,
And the hours and moments like minutes pass.

Stevie Smith (1902–1971)

To the Same

TO A FRIEND

We parted on the mountains, as two streams
From one clear spring pursue their several ways;
And thy fleet course hath been through many a maze
In foreign lands, where silvery Padus gleams
To that delicious sky, whose glowing beams
Brighten'd the tresses that old Poets praise;
Where Petrarch's patient love and artful lays,
And Ariosto's song of many themes,
Moved the soft air. But I, a lazy brook,
As close pent up within my native dell,
Have crept along from nook to shady nook,
Where flowerets blow, and whispering Naiads dwell.
Yet now we met, that parted were so wide,
O'er rough and smooth to travel side by side.

Hartley Coleridge (1796–1849)

Meeting at Night

I

The grey sea and the long black land;
And the yellow half-moon large and low;
And the startled little waves that leap
In fiery ringlets from their sleep,
As I gain the cove with pushing prow,
And quench its speed in the slushy sand.

II

Then a mile of warm sea-scented beach;
Three fields to cross till a farm appears;
A tap at the pane, the quick sharp scratch
And blue spurt of a lighted match,
And a voice less loud, thro' its joys and fears,
Than the two hearts beating each to each!

Robert Browning (1812–1889)

Silence

'Tis better to sit here beside the sea,
Here on the spray-kissed beach,
In silence, that between such friends as we
Is full of deepest speech.

Paul Laurence Dunbar (1872–1906)

I'm Thankful That My Life Doth Not Deceive

I'm thankful that my life doth not deceive
Itself with a low loftiness, half height,
And think it soars when still it dip its way
Beneath the clouds on noiseless pinion
Like the crow or owl, but it doth know
The full extent of all its trivialness,
Compared with the splendid heights above.
See how it waits to watch the mail come in
While 'hind its back the sun goes out perchance.
And yet their lumbering cart brings me no word,
Not one scrawled leaf such as my neighbors get
To cheer them with the slight events forsooth,
Faint ups and downs of their far distant friends –
And now 'tis passed. What next? See the long train
Of teams wreathed in dust, their atmosphere;
Shall I attend until the last is passed?
Else why these ears that hear the leader's bells
Or eyes that link me in procession?
But hark! the drowsy day has done its task,
Far in yon hazy field where stands a barn,
Unanxious hens improve the sultry hour
And with contented voice now brag their deed –
A new laid egg – Now let the day decline –
They'll lay another by tomorrow's sun.

Henry David Thoreau (1817–1862)

Pirate Story

Three of us afloat in the meadow by the swing,
  Three of us aboard in the basket on the lea.
Winds are in the air, they are blowing in the spring,
  And waves are on the meadows like the waves there are at sea.

Where shall we adventure, to-day that we're afloat,
  Wary of the weather and steering by a star?
Shall it be to Africa, a-steering of the boat,
  To Providence, or Babylon, or off to Malabar?

Hi! but here's a squadron a-rowing on the sea –
  Cattle on the meadow a-charging with a roar!
Quick, and we'll escape them, they're as mad as they can be
  The wicket is the harbour and the garden is the shore.

Robert Louis Stevenson (1850–1894)

25 AUGUST

A Time to Talk

When a friend calls to me from the road
And slows his horse to a meaning walk,
I don't stand still and look around
On all the hills I haven't hoed,
And shout from where I am, 'What is it?'
No, not as there is a time to talk.
I thrust my hoe in the mellow ground,
Blade-end up and five feet tall,
And plod: I go up to the stone wall
For a friendly visit.

Robert Frost (1874–1963)

She Walks in Beauty

I

She walks in beauty, like the night
Of cloudless climes and starry skies;
And all that's best of dark and bright
Meet in her aspect and her eyes;
Thus mellowed to that tender light
Which heaven to gaudy day denies.

II

One shade the more, one ray the less,
Had half impair'd the nameless grace
Which waves in every raven tress,
Or softly lightens o'er her face;
Where thoughts serenely sweet express,
How pure, how dear their dwelling-place.

III

And on that cheek, and o'er that brow,
So soft, so calm, yet eloquent,
The smiles that win, the tints that glow,
But tell of days in goodness spent,
A mind at peace with all below,
A heart whose love is innocent!

George Gordon, Lord Byron (1788–1824)

The Lark Now Leaves His Watery Nest

The lark now leaves his watery nest,
  And climbing shakes his dewy wings;
He takes your window for the East,
  And to implore your light, he sings:
Awake, awake! the morn will never rise
Till she can dress her beauty at your eyes.

The merchant bows unto the seaman's star,
  The ploughman from the sun his season takes;
But still the lover wonders what they are
  Who look for day before his mistress wakes:
Awake, awake! break through your veils of lawn;
Then draw your curtains, and begin the dawn!

Sir William Davenant (1606–1668)

All Paths Lead to You

All paths lead to you
  Where e'er I stray,
You are the evening star
  At the end of the day.

All paths lead to you
  Hill-top or low,
You are the white birch
  In the sun's glow.

All paths lead to you
  Where e'er I roam
You are the lark-song
  Calling me home!

Blanche Shoemaker Wagstaff (1888–1959)

Sonnet CIV

To me, fair friend, you never can be old,
For as you were when first your eye I eyed,
Such seems your beauty still. Three winters cold
Have from the forests shook three summers' pride,
Three beauteous springs to yellow autumn turned
In process of the seasons have I seen,
Three April perfumes in three hot Junes burned,
Since first I saw you fresh, which yet are green.
Ah, yet doth beauty, like a dial hand,
Steal from his figure, and no pace perceived;
So your sweet hue, which methinks still doth stand,
Hath motion, and mine eye may be deceived:
  For fear of which, hear this, thou age unbred:
  Ere you were born was beauty's summer dead.

William Shakespeare (1564–1616)

O Sweet Delight

O sweet delight, O more then humane blisse,
With her to live that ever loving is;
To heare her speake, whose words so well are plac't,
That she by them, as they in her are grac't;
  Those lookes to view that feast the viewers eye;
  How blest is he that may so live and dye!

Such love as this the golden times did know,
When all did reape, yet none tooke care to sow:
Such love as this an endlesse Summer makes,
And all distaste from fraile affection takes.
  So lov'd, so blest, in my belov'd am I;
  Which till their eyes ake, let yron men envy

Thomas Campion (1567–1620)

Song

1

Soft falls the sweet evening
  Bright shines the one star
The night clouds they're leaning
  On mountains afar
The moon in dim brightness
  The fern in its lightness
Tinge the valley with whiteness
Both near and far

2

O soft falls the evening
  Around those sweet glens
The hill's shadows leaning
  Half over the glen
There meet me my deary
  I'm lonely and weary
And nothing can cheer me
  So meet me agen

3

The gate it clap'd slightly
  The noise it was small
The footstep fell lightly
  And she pass'd the stone wall
And is it my deary
  I'm no longer weary
But happy and cheery
  For in thee I meet all

John Clare (1793–1864)

SEPTEMBER

Such Sweet Company

By the Seaside: Dedication

As one who, walking in the twilight gloom,
  Hears round about him voices as it darkens,
And seeing not the forms from which they come,
  Pauses from time to time, and turns and hearkens;

So walking here in twilight, O my friends!
  I hear your voices, softened by the distance,
And pause, and turn to listen, as each sends
  His words of friendship, comfort, and assistance.

If any thought of mine, or sung or told,
  Has ever given delight or consolation,
Ye have repaid me back a thousand-fold,
  By every friendly sign and salutation.

Thanks for the sympathies that ye have shown!
  Thanks for each kindly word, each silent token,
That teaches me, when seeming most alone,
  Friends are around us, though no word be spoken.

Kind messages, that pass from land to land;
  Kind letters, that betray the heart's deep history,
In which we feel the pressure of a hand, –
One touch of fire, – and all the rest is mystery!

The pleasant books, that silently among
  Our household treasures take familiar places,
And are to us as if a living tongue
  Spice from the printed leaves or pictured faces!

Perhaps on earth I never shall behold,
  With eye of sense, your outward form and semblance;
Therefore to me ye never will grow old,
  But live forever young in my remembrance!

Never grow old, nor change, nor pass away!
  Your gentle voices will flow on forever,
When life grows bare and tarnished with decay,
  As through a leafless landscape flows a river.

Not chance of birth or place has made us friends,
  Being oftentimes of different tongues and nations,
But the endeavor for the selfsame ends,
  With the same hopes, and fears, and aspirations.

Therefore I hope to join your seaside walk,
  Saddened, and mostly silent, with emotion;
Not interrupting with intrusive talk
  The grand, majestic symphonies of ocean.

Therefore I hope, as no unwelcome guest,
At your warm fireside, when the lamps are lighted,
To have my place reserved among the rest,
Nor stand as one unsought and uninvited!

Henry Wadsworth Longfellow (1807–1882)

Neighbours

The man that is open of heart to his neighbour,
And stops to consider his likes and dislikes,
His blood shall be wholesome whatever his labour,
His luck shall be with him whatever he strikes.
The Splendour of Morning shall duly possess him,
That he may not be sad at the falling of eve.
And, when he has done with mere living – God bless him! –
A many shall sigh, and one Woman shall grieve!

But he that is costive of soul toward his fellow,
Through the ways, and the works, and the woes of this life,
Him food shall not fatten, him drink shall not mellow;
And his innards shall brew him perpetual strife.
His eye shall be blind to God's Glory above him;
His ear shall be deaf to Earth's Laughter around;
His Friends and his Club and his Dog shall not love him;
And his Widow shall skip when he goes underground!

Rudyard Kipling (1865–1936)

First Love

I ne'er was struck before that hour
  With love so sudden and so sweet
Her face it bloomed like a sweet flower
  And stole my heart away complete
My face turned pale as deadly pale
  My legs refused to walk away
And when she looked, what could I ail
  My life and all seemed turned to clay

And then my blood rushed to my face
  And took my eyesight quite away
The trees and bushes round the place
  Seemed midnight at noonday
I could not see a single thing
  Words from my eyes did start
They spoke as chords do from the string
  And blood burnt round my heart

Are flowers the winter's choice
  Is love's bed always snow
She seemed to hear my silent voice
  Not love's appeals to know
I never saw so sweet a face
  As that I stood before
My heart has left its dwelling-place
  And can return no more –

John Clare (1793–1864)

As I Walked Out One Evening

VERSES 1–5

As I walked out one evening,
  Walking down Bristol Street,
The crowds upon the pavement
  Were fields of harvest wheat.

And down by the brimming river
  I heard a lover sing
Under an arch of the railway:
  'Love has no ending.

'I'll love you, dear, I'll love you
  Till China and Africa meet,
And the river jumps over the mountain
  And the salmon sing in the street,

'I'll love you till the ocean
  Is folded and hung up to dry
And the seven stars go squawking
  Like geese about the sky.

'The years shall run like rabbits,
  For in my arms I hold
The Flower of the Ages,
  And the first love of the world.'

W. H. Auden (1907–1973)

Birthday

My heart is like a singing bird
  Whose nest is in a watered shoot;
My heart is like an apple-tree
  Whose boughs are bent with thickset fruit;
My heart is like a rainbow shell
  That paddles in a halcyon sea;
My heart is gladder than all these
  Because my love is come to me.

Raise me a dais of silk and down;
  Hang it with vair and purple dyes;
Carve it in doves and pomegranates,
  And peacocks with a hundred eyes;
Work it in gold and silver grapes,
  In leaves and silver fleurs-de-lys;
Because the birthday of my life
  Is come, my love is come to me.

Christina Rossetti (1830–1894)

Friendship

A ruddy drop of manly blood
The surging sea outweighs,
The world uncertain comes and goes;
The lover rooted stays.
I fancied he was fled, –
And, after many a year,
Glowed unexhausted kindliness,
Like daily sunrise there.
My careful heart was free again,
O friend, my bosom said,
Through thee alone the sky is arched,
Through thee the rose is red;
All things through thee take nobler form,
And look beyond the earth,
The mill-round of our fate appears
A sun-path in thy worth.
Me too thy nobleness has taught
To master my despair;
The fountains of my hidden life
Are through thy friendship fair.

Ralph Waldo Emerson (1803–1882)

To Mrs M. A. at Parting

VERSES 1–4

I have examin'd and do find,
        Of all that favour me,
There's none I grieve to leave behind
        But only, only thee.
To part with thee I needs must die,
Could parting sep'rate thee and I.

But neither Chance nor Compliment
        Did element our Love:
'Twas sacred Sympathy was lent
        Us from the quire above.
That Friendship Fortune did create,
Still fears a wound from Time or Fate.

Our chang'd and mingled souls are grown
        To such acquaintance now,
That if each would resume their own,
        Alas! We know not how.
We have each other so engrost,
That each is in the union lost.

And thus we can no Absence know,
    Nor shall we be confin'd;
Our active souls will daily go
    To learn each other's mind
Nay, should we never meet to Sense,
Our souls would hold Intelligence.

Katherine Philips (1632–1664)

Sonnet LXXV

FROM *AMORETTI*

One day I wrote her name upon the strand,
    But came the waves and washed it away:
    Again I wrote it with a second hand,
    But came the tide, and made my pains his prey.
Vain man, said she, that dost in vain assay,
    A mortal thing so to immortalize
    For I myself shall like to this decay,
    And eke my name be wiped out likewise.
Not so, (quod I) let baser things devise
    To die in dust, but you shall live by fame:
    My verse your vertues rare shall eternize,
    And in the heavens write your glorious name:
Where whereas Death shall all the world subdue,
    Our love shall live, and later life renew.

Edmund Spenser (c.1552–1599)

A Quoi Bon Dire

Seventeen years ago you said
Something that sounded like Good-bye;
And everybody thinks that you are dead,
But I.

So I, as I grow stiff and cold
To this and that say Good-bye too;
And everybody sees that I am old
But you.

And one fine morning in a sunny lane
Some boy and girl will meet and kiss and swear
That nobody can love their way again
While over there
You will have smiled, I shall have tossed your hair.

Charlotte Mew (1869–1928)

Friendship

Though love may be deeper, Friendship is more wide;
Like some high plateau stretching limitless,
It may not feel the ultimate caress
Of sun-kissed peaks, remote and glorified.
But here the light, with gentler winds allied.
The broad horizon sweeps, till loneliness.
The cruel tyrant of the Soul's distress.
In such sweet company may not abide.
Friendship has vision, though dear Love be blind.
And swift and full communion in the fair
Free flights of high and sudden ecstasy,
The broad excursions where, mind knit to mind.
And heart by heart renewed, can all things dare
Lit by the fire of perfect sympathy.

Corinne Roosevelt Robinson (1861–1933)

Friendship

LINES 1–48

What virtue or what mental grace,
But men unqualified and base
  Will boast it their possession?
Profusion apes the noble part
Of liberality of heart,
  And dullness of discretion.

If ev'ry polish'd gem we find,
Illuminating heart or mind,
  Provoke to imitation;
No wonder friendship does the same,
That jewel of the purest flame,
  Or rather constellation.

No knave but boldly will pretend
The requisites that form a friend,
  A real and a sound one,
Nor any fool he would deceive,
But proves as ready to believe,
  And dreams that he had found one.

Candid and generous and just,
Boys care but little whom they trust.
  An error soon corrected –
For who but learns in riper years,
That man, when smoothest he appears,
  Is most to be suspected?

But here again a danger lies,
Lest, having misapplied our eyes,
  And taken trash for treasure,
We should unwarily conclude
Friendship a false ideal good,
  A mere Utopian pleasure.

An acquisition rather rare
Is yet no subject of despair;
  Nor is it wise complaining,
If either on forbidden ground,
Or where it was not to be found,
  We sought without attaining.

No friendship will abide the test,
That stands on sordid interest,
  Or mean self-love erected;
Nor such as may awhile subsist
Between the sot and sensualist,
  For vicious ends connected.

Who seeks a friend, should come dispos'd
T' exhibit, in full bloom disclos'd,
  The graces and the beauties
That form the character he seeks,
For 'tis a union that bespeaks
  Reciprocated duties.

William Cowper (1731–1800)

Love Poem

I live in you, you live in me;
We are two gardens haunted by each other.
Sometimes I cannot find you there,
There is only the swing creaking, that you have just left,
Or your favourite book beside the sundial.

Douglas Dunn (1942–)

Love's Philosophy

I

The fountains mingle with the river
  And the rivers with the Ocean,
The winds of Heaven mix for ever
  With a sweet emotion;
Nothing in the world is single;
  All things by a law divine
In one spirit meet and mingle.
  Why not I with thine? –

II

See the mountains kiss high Heaven
  And the waves clasp one another;
No sister-flower would be forgiven
  If it disdained its brother;
And the sunlight clasps the earth
  And the moonbeams kiss the sea:
What is all this sweet work worth
  If thou kiss not me?

Percy Bysshe Shelley (1792–1822)

XXVII

FROM *IN MEMORIAM A. H. H.*

I envy not in any moods
    The captive void of noble rage,
    The linnet born within the cage,
That never knew the summer woods:

I envy not the beast that takes
    His license in the field of time,
    Unfettered by the sense of crime,
To whom a conscience never wakes;

Nor, what may count itself as blest,
    The heart that never plighted troth
    But stagnates in the weeds of sloth;
Nor any want-begotten rest.

I hold it true, what e'er befall;
    I feel it when I sorrow most;
    'Tis better to have loved and lost
Than never to have loved at all.

Alfred, Lord Tennyson (1809–1892)

15 SEPTEMBER

A Friendly Welcome

FROM *DON JUAN*, CANTO I, CXXIII

'Tis sweet to hear the watchdog's honest bark
Bay deep-mouth'd welcome as we draw near home;
'Tis sweet to know there is an eye will mark
Our coming, and look brighter when we come.

George Gordon, Lord Byron (1788–1824)

Friendship

I think awhile of Love, and while I think,
  Love is to me a world,
  Sole meat and sweetest drink,
  And close connecting link
    Tween heaven and earth.

I only know it is, not how or why,
  My greatest happiness;
  However hard I try,
  Not if I were to die,
    Can I explain.

I fain would ask my friend how it can be,
  But when the time arrives,
  Then Love is more lovely
  Than anything to me,
    And so I'm dumb.

For if the truth were known, Love cannot speak,
  But only thinks and does;
  Though surely out 'twill leak
  Without the help of Greek,
    Or any tongue.

A man may love the truth and practise it,
    Beauty he may admire,
  And goodness not omit,
  As much as may befit
    To reverence.

But only when these three together meet,
As they always incline,
  And make one soul the seat,
  And favorite retreat,
    Of loveliness;

When under kindred shape, like loves and hates
  And a kindred nature,
  Proclaim us to be mates,
  Exposed to equal fates
    Eternally;

And each may other help, and service do,
  Drawing Love's bands more tight,
  Service he ne'er shall rue
  While one and one make two,
    And two are one;

In such case only doth man fully prove
  Fully as man can do,
  What power there is in Love
  His inmost soul to move
    Resistlessly.

Two sturdy oaks I mean, which side by side,
  Withstand the winter's storm,
  And spite of wind and tide,
  Grow up the meadow's pride,
    For both are strong.

Above they barely touch, but undermined
  Down to their deepest source,
  Admiring you shall find
  Their roots are intertwined
    Insep'rably.

Henry David Thoreau (1817–1862)

Inviting a Friend to Supper

To night, grave sir, both my poore house, and I
Doe equally desire your companie:
Not that we thinke us worthy such a ghest,
But that your worth will dignifie our feast,
With those that come; whose grace may make that seeme
Something, which else, could hope for no esteeme.
It is the faire acceptance, Sir, creates
The entertaynment perfect: not the cates.
Yet shall you have, to rectifie your palate,
An olive, capers, or some better sallade
Ushring the mutton; with a short-leg'd hen,
If we can get her, full of egs, and then
Limons, and wine for sauce: to these a coney
Is not to be despair'd of, for our money;
And, though fowle, now, be scarce, yet there are clarkes,
The skie not falling, thinke we may have larkes.
Ile tell you more, and lye, so you will come:
Of partrich, pheasant, wood-cock, of which some
May yet be there; and godwit, if we can:
Knat, raile, and ruffe too. How so ere, my man
Shall reade a piece of Virgil, Tacitus,
Livie, or of some better booke to us,
Of which wee'll speak our minds, amidst our meate;
And Ile professe no verses to repeate:
To this, if ought appeare which I not know of,
That will the pastrie, not my paper, show of.
Digestive cheese and fruit there sure will bee;
But that, which most doth take my Muse and mee,

Is a pure cup of rich Canary-wine,
Which is the Mermaids now, but shall be mine:
Of which had Horace, or Anacreon tasted,
Their lives, as doe their lines, till now had lasted.
Tobacco, Nectar, or the Thespian spring,
Are all but Luthers beere to this I sing.
Of this we will sup free, but moderately,
And we will have no Pooly, or Parrot by;
Nor shall our cups make any guiltie men;
But, at our parting we will be, as when
We innocently met. No simple word,
That shall be utter'd at our mirthfull boord,
Shall make us sad next morning: or affright
The libertie that wee'll enjoy to night.

Ben Jonson (c.1572–1637)

My Cat Jeoffrey

FROM *JUBILATE AGNO*, LINES 1–34

For I will consider my Cat Jeoffry.
For he is the servant of the Living God duly and daily
  serving him.
For at the first glance of the glory of God in the East he
  worships in his way.
For this is done by wreathing his body seven times round
  with elegant quickness.
For then he leaps up to catch the musk, which is the
  blessing of God upon his prayer.
For he rolls upon prank to work it in.
For having done duty and received blessing he begins to
  consider himself.
For this he performs in ten degrees.
For first he looks upon his fore-paws to see if they are
  clean.
For secondly he kicks up behind to clear away there.
For thirdly he works it upon stretch with the fore-paws
  extended.
For fourthly he sharpens his paws by wood.
For fifthly he washes himself.
For sixthly he rolls upon wash.
For seventhly he fleas himself, that he may not be
  interrupted upon the beat.
For eighthly he rubs himself against a post.
For ninthly he looks up for his instructions.
For tenthly he goes in quest of food.
For having consider'd God and himself he will consider his
  neighbour.

For if he meets another cat he will kiss her in kindness.
For when he takes his prey he plays with it to give it a chance.
For one mouse in seven escapes by his dallying.
For when his day's work is done his business more properly begins.
For he keeps the Lord's watch in the night against the adversary.
For he counteracts the powers of darkness by his electrical skin and glaring eyes.
For he counteracts the Devil, who is death, by brisking about the life.
For in his morning orisons he loves the sun and the sun loves him.
For he is of the tribe of Tiger.
For the Cherub Cat is a term of the Angel Tiger.
For he has the subtlety and hissing of a serpent, which in goodness he suppresses.
For he will not do destruction, if he is well-fed, neither will he spit without provocation.
For he purrs in thankfulness, when God tells him he's a good Cat.
For he is an instrument for the children to learn benevolence upon.
For every house is incomplete without him and a blessing is lacking in the spirit.

Christopher Smart (1722–1771)

The Precise Moment When Friendship is Formed

FROM *THE LIFE OF SAMUEL JOHNSON*

We cannot tell the precise moment when friendship is formed. As in filling a vessel drop by drop, there is at last a drop which makes it run over; so in a series of kindnesses there is at last one which makes the heart run over.

James Boswell (1740–1795)

Friendship

FROM *THE FAIR PENITENT*

Lavinia:

Be gay again, and know the Joys of Friendship
The Trust, Security, and mutual Tenderness,
The double Joys, where each is glad for both;
  Friendship,
Friendship, the Wealth, the last Retreat and Strength.
Secure against ill Fortune, and the World.

Nicholas Rowe (1674–1718)

To E. Fitzgerald

Old Fitz, who from your suburb grange,
    Where once I tarried for a while,
Glance at the wheeling Orb of change,
    And greet it with a kindly smile;
Whom yet I see as there you sit
    Beneath your sheltering garden-tree,
And watch your doves about you flit,
    And plant on shoulder, hand, and knee,
Or on your head their rosy feet,
    As if they knew your diet spares
Whatever moved in that full sheet
    Let down to Peter at his prayers;
Who live on milk and meal and grass;
    And once for ten long weeks I tried
Your table of Pythagoras,
    And seem'd at first 'a thing enskied,'
(As Shakespeare has it) airy-light
    To float above the ways of men,
Then fell from that half-spiritual height
    Chill'd, till I tasted flesh again
One night when earth was winter-black,
    And all the heavens flash'd in frost;
And on me, half-asleep, came back
    That wholesome heat the blood had lost,
And set me climbing icy capes
    And glaciers, over which there roll'd
To meet me long-arm'd vines with grapes
    Of Eshcol hugeness; for the cold
Without, and warmth within me, wrought

To mould the dream; but none can say
That Lenten fare makes Lenten thought
Who reads your golden Eastern lay,
Than which I know no version done
In English more divinely well;
A planet equal to the sun
Which cast it, that large infidel
Your Omar, and your Omar drew
Full-handed plaudits from our best
In modern letters, and from two,
Old friends outvaluing all the rest,
Two voices heard on earth no more;
But we old friends are still alive,
And I am nearing seventy-four,
While you have touch'd at seventy-five,
And so I send a birthday line
Of greeting; and my son, who dipt
In some forgotten book of mine
With sallow scraps of manuscript,
And dating many a year ago,
Has hit on this, which you will take,
My Fitz, and welcome, as I know,
Less for its own than for the sake
Of one recalling gracious times,
When, in our younger London days,
You found some merit in my rhymes,
And I more pleasure in your praise.

Alfred, Lord Tennyson (1809–1892)

Being Her Friend

Being her friend, I do not care, not I,
How gods or men may wrong me, beat me down;
Her word's sufficient star to travel by,
I count her quiet praise sufficient crown.

Being her friend, I do not covet gold,
Save a royal gift to give her pleasure;
To sit with her, and have her hand to hold,
Is wealth, I think, surpassing minted treasure.

Being her friend, I only covet art,
A white pure flame to search me as I trace
In crooked letters from a throbbing heart
The hymn to beauty written on her face.

John Masefield (1878–1967)

Sonnet: I Thank You

I thank you, kind and best beloved friend,
With the same thanks one murmurs to a sister,
When, for some gentle favor, he hath kissed her,
Less for the gifts than for the love you send,
Less for the flowers, than what the flowers convey;
If I, indeed, divine their meaning truly,
And not unto myself ascribe, unduly,
Things which you neither meant nor wished to say,
Oh! tell me, is the hope then all misplaced?
And am I flattered by my own affection?
But in your beauteous gift, methought I traced
Something above a short-lived predilection,
And which, for that I know no dearer name,
I designate as love, without love's flame.

Henry Timrod (1829–1867)

Destiny

Somewhere there waiteth in this world of ours
  For one lone soul another lonely soul –
Each choosing each through all the weary hours,
  And meeting strangely at one sudden goal;
Then blend they – like green leaves with golden flowers,
  Into one beautiful and perfect whole –
And life's long night is ended, and the way
  Lies open onward to eternal day.

Sir Edwin Arnold (1832–1904)

The Means to Attain a Happy Life

Martial, the things that do attain
The happy life be these, I find:
The riches left, not got with pain,
The fruitful ground; the quiet mind;

The equal friend; no grudge, no strife;
No charge of rule nor governance;
Without disease the healthy life;
The household of continuance;

The mean diet, no dainty fare;
True wisdom joined with simpleness;
The night discharged of all care,
Where wine the wit may not oppress;

The faithful wife, without debate;
Such sleeps as may beguile the night:
Content thyself with thine estate,
Neither wish death, nor fear his might.

Henry Howard, Earl of Surrey (1517–1547)

I Wish I Could Remember

'ERA GIÀ L'ORA CHE VOLGE IL DESIO.' – DANTE
'RICORRO AL TEMPO CH'IO VI VIDI PRIMA.' – PETRARCA
FROM *MONNA INNOMINATA: A SONNET OF SONNETS*

I wish I could remember that first day,
First hour, first moment of your meeting me,
If bright or dim the season, it might be
Summer or Winter for aught I can say;
So unrecorded did it slip away,
So blind was I to see and to foresee,
So dull to mark the budding of my tree
That would not blossom yet for many a May.
If only I could recollect it, such
A day of days! I let it come and go
As traceless as a thaw of bygone snow;
It seemed to mean so little, meant so much;
If only now I could recall that touch,
First touch of hand in hand – Did one but know!

Christina Rossetti (1830–1894)

For her Gait, if she be Walking

For her gait, if she be walking;
Be she sitting, I desire her
For her state's sake; and admire her
For her wit if she be talking;
    Gait and state and wit approve her;
    For which all and each I love her.
Be she sullen, I commend her
For a modest. Be she merry,
For a kind one her prefer I.
Briefly, everything doth lend her
    So much grace, and so approve her,
    That for everything I love her.

William Browne (c.1591–c.1645)

Reprise

Geniuses of countless nations
Have told their love for generations
Till all their memorable phrases
Are common as goldenrod or daisies.
Their girls have glimmered like the moon,
Or shimmered like a summer moon,
Stood like a lily, fled like a fawn,
Now the sunset, now the dawn,
Here the princess in the tower
There the sweet forbidden flower.
Darling, when I look at you
Every aged phrase is new,
And there are moments when it seems
I've married one of Shakespeare's dreams.

Ogden Nash (1902–1971)

If You Were Coming in the Fall

If you were coming in the Fall,
I'd brush the Summer by
With half a smile, and half a spurn,
As Housewives do, a Fly.

If I could see you in a year,
I'd wind the months in balls –
And put them each in separate Drawers,
For fear the numbers fuse –

If only Centuries, delayed,
I'd count them on my Hand,
Subtracting, till my fingers dropped
Into Van Dieman's Land,

If certain, when this life was out –
That yours and mine, should be
I'd toss it yonder, like a Rind,
And take Eternity –

But, now, uncertain of the length
Of this, that is between,
It goads me, like the Goblin Bee –
That will not state – its sting.

Emily Dickinson (1830–1886)

Summer Friends

The Swallow is a summer bird;
  He in our chimneys, when the weather
Is fine and warm, may then be heard
  Chirping his notes for weeks together.

Come there but one cold wintry day,
  Away will fly our guest the Swallow:
And much like him we find the way
  Which many a gay young friend will follow.

In dreary days of snow and frost
  Closer to Man will cling the Sparrow:
Old friends, although in life we're crost,
  Their hearts to us will never narrow.

Give me the bird – 'give me the friend –
  Will sing in frost – will love in sorrow –
Whate'er mischance to-day may send,
  Will greet me with his sight to-morrow.

Mary Lamb (1764–1847)

OCTOBER

In Sunshine and in Shade

Marriage Morning

Light, so low upon earth,
  You send a flash to the sun.
Here is the golden close of love,
  All my wooing is done.
Oh, all the woods and the meadows,
  Woods, where we hid from the wet,
Stiles where we stayed to be kind,
  Meadows in which we met!
Light, so low in the vale
  You flash and lighten afar,
For this is the golden morning of love,
  And you are his morning star.
Flash, I am coming, I come,
  By meadow and stile and wood,
Oh, lighten into my eyes and my heart,
  Into my heart and my blood!
Heart, are you great enough
  For a love that never tires?
O heart, are you great enough for love?
  I have heard of thorns and briers.
Over the thorns and briers,
  Over the meadows and stiles,
Over the world to the end of it
  Flash of a million miles.

Alfred, Lord Tennyson (1809–1892)

The Friend Who Just Stands By

When trouble comes your soul to try,
You love the friend who just 'stands by.'
Perhaps there's nothing he can do –
The thing is strictly up to you;
For there are troubles all your own,
And paths the soul must tread alone;
Times when love cannot smooth the road
Nor friendship lift the heavy load,
But just to know you have a friend
Who will 'stand by' until the end,
Whose sympathy through all endures,
Whose warm handclasp is always yours –
It helps, someway, to pull you through,
Although there's nothing he can do.
And so with fervent heart you cry,
'God bless the friend who just "stands by"!'

B. Y. Williams (?–1951)

Travelling

This is the spot: – how mildly does the sun
Shine in between the fading leaves! the air
In the habitual silence of this wood
Is more than silent: and this bed of heath,
Where shall we find so sweet a resting-place?
Come! – let me see thee sink into a dream
Of quiet thoughts, – protracted till thine eye
Be calm as water, when the winds are gone
And no one can tell whither. – my sweet friend!
We two have had such happy hours together
That my heart melts in me to think of it.

William Wordsworth (1770–1850)

Friends

Now must I these three praise –
Three women that have wrought
What joy is in my days:
One because no thought,
Nor those unpassing cares,
No, not in these fifteen
Many-times-troubled years,
Could ever come between
Mind and delighted mind;
And one because her hand
Had strength that could unbind
What none can understand,
What none can have and thrive,
Youth's dreamy load, till she
So changed me that I live
Labouring in ecstasy.
And what of her that took
All till my youth was gone
With scarce a pitying look?
How could I praise that one?
When day begins to break

I count my good and bad,
Being wakeful for her sake,
Remembering what she had,
What eagle look still shows,
While up from my heart's root
So great a sweetness flows
I shake from head to foot.

W. B. Yeats (1865–1939)

XLIII

FROM *SONNETS FROM THE PORTUGUESE*

How do I love thee? Let me count the ways.
I love thee to the depth and breadth and height
My soul can reach, when feeling out of sight
For the ends of Being and ideal Grace.
I love thee to the level of everyday's
Most quiet need, by sun and candle-light.
I love thee freely, as men strive for Right;
I love thee purely, as they turn from Praise.
I love thee with the passion put to use
In my old griefs, and with my childhood's faith.
I love thee with a love I seemed to lose
With my lost saints, – I love thee with the breath,
Smiles, tears, of all my life! – and, if God choose,
I shall but love thee better after death.

Elizabeth Barrett Browning (1806–1861)

A Kindly Neighbor

I have a kindly neighbor, one who stands
Beside my gate and chats with me awhile,
Gives me the glory of his radiant smile
And comes at times to help with willing hands.
No station high or rank this man commands;
He, too, must trudge, as I, the long day's mile;
And yet, devoid of pomp or gaudy style,
He has a worth exceeding stocks or lands.

To him I go when sorrow's at my door;
On him I lean when burdens come my way;
Together oft we talk our trials o'er
And there is warmth in each good-night we say.
A kindly neighbor! Wars and strife shall end
When man has made the man next door his friend.

Edgar Guest (1881–1959)

XXXIII

FROM *A SHROPSHIRE LAD*

If truth in hearts that perish
        Could move the powers on high,
I think the love I bear you
        Should make you not to die.

Sure, sure, if stedfast meaning,
        If single thought could save,
The world might end to-morrow,
        You should not see the grave.

This long and sure-set liking,
        This boundless will to please,
– Oh, you should live for ever,
        If there were help in these.

But now, since all is idle,
        To this lost heart be kind,
Ere to a town you journey
        Where friends are ill to find.

A. E. Housman (1859–1936)

Hero amd Leander

FROM *SESTIAD I*, LINES 167–176

It lies not in our power to love or hate,
For will in us is overruled by fate.
When two are stripped, long ere the course begin,
We wish that one should lose, the other win;
And one especially do we affect
Of two gold ingots, like in each respect.
The reason no man knows: let it suffice,
What we behold is censured by our eyes.
Where both deliberate, the love is slight;
Who ever loved, that loved not at first sight?

Christopher Marlowe (1564–1593)

Friendship

And a youth said, Speak to us of Friendship.
And he answered, saying:
Your friend is your needs answered.
He is your field which you sow with love and reap with thanksgiving.
And he is your board and your fireside.
For you come to him with your hunger, and you seek him for peace.

When your friend speaks his mind you fear not the "nay" in your own mind, nor do you withhold the 'ay.'
And when he is silent your heart ceases not to listen to his heart;
For without words, in friendship, all thoughts, all desires, all expectations are born and shared, with joy that is unacclaimed.
When you part from your friend you grieve not;
For that which you love most in him may be clearer in his absence, as the mountain to the climber is clearer from the plain.

And let there be no purpose in friendship save the deepening of the spirit.
For love that seeks aught but the disclosure of its own mystery is not love but a net cast forth: and only the unprofitable is caught.

And let your best be for your friend.
If he must know the ebb of your tide, let him know its flood also.

For what is your friend that you should seek him with hours to kill?
Seek him always with hours to live.
For it is his to fill your need, but not your emptiness.
And in the sweetness of friendship let there be laughter, and sharing of pleasures.
For in the dew of little things the heart finds its morning and is refreshed.

Kahlil Gibran (1883–1931)

10 OCTOBER

Friendship

FROM *TO MR HENRY LAWES*

Beauty is but composure, and we find
Content is but the concord of the mind,
Friendship the unison of well-turned hearts,
Honor the chorus of the noblest parts,
And all the world on which we can reflect
Music to th'ear, or to the intellect.

Katherine Philips (1632–1664)

We Have Been Friends Together

We have been friends together,
In sunshine and in shade;
Since first beneath the chestnut trees
In infancy we played.
But coldness dwells within thy heart,
A cloud is on thy brow;
We have been friends together –
Shall a light word part us now?

We have been gay together;
We have laugh'd at little jests;
For the fount of hope was gushing
Warm and joyous in our breasts.
But laughter now hath fled thy lip,
And sullen glooms thy brow;
We have been gay together –
Shall a light word part us now?

We have been sad together,
We have wept, with bitter tears,
O'er the grass-grown graves, where slumber'd
The hopes of early years.
The voices which are silent there
Would bid thee clear thy brow;
We have been sad together—
Oh! what shall part us now?

Caroline Elizabeth Sarah Norton (1808–1877)

LVII

FROM *A SHROPSHIRE LAD*

You smile upon your friend to-day,
  To-day his ills are over;
You hearken to the lover's say,
  And happy is the lover.

'Tis late to hearken, late to smile,
  But better late than never:
I shall have lived a little while
  Before I die for ever.

A. E. Housman (1859–1936)

Friendship

Thou that hast giv'n so much to me,
Give one thing more, a grateful heart.
See how thy beggar works on thee
By art.

He makes thy gifts occasion more,
And says, If he in this be crost,
All thou hast giv'n him heretofore
Is lost.

But thou didst reckon, when at first
Thy word our hearts and hands did crave,
What it would come to at the worst
To save.

Perpetual knockings at thy door,
Tears sullying thy transparent rooms,
Gift upon gift, much would have more,

And comes.
This notwithstanding, thou wentst on,
And didst allow us all our noise:
Nay thou hast made a sigh and groan
Thy joys.

Not that thou hast not still above
Much better tunes, than groans can make;
But that these country-airs thy love
Did take.

Wherefore I cry, and cry again;
And in no quiet canst thou be,
Till I a thankful heart obtain
Of thee:

Not thankful, when it pleaseth me;
As if thy blessings had spare days:
But such a heart, whose pulse may be
Thy praise.

George Herbert (1593–1633)

The Kiss

'I saw you take his kiss!' ' 'Tis true.'
  'O, modesty!' ''Twas strictly kept:
He thought me asleep; at least I knew
He thought I thought he thought I slept.'

Coventry Patmore (1823–1896)

An Epistle to Master Arthur Squib

What I am not, and what I faine would be,
Whilst I informe my selfe, I would teach thee,
My gentle Arthur; that it might be said
One lesson we have both learn'd, and well read;
I neither am, nor art thou one of those
That hearkens to a Jacks-pulse, when it goes.
Nor ever trusted to that friendship yet
Was issue of the Taverne, or the Spit:
Much lesse a name would we bring up, or nurse,
That could but claime a kindred from the purse.
Those are poore Ties, depend on those false ends,
'Tis vertue alone, or nothing that knits friends:
And as within your Office, you do take
No piece of money, but you know, or make
Inquirie of the worth: So must we doe,
First weigh a friend, then touch, and trie him too:
For there are many slips, and Counterfeits.
Deceit is fruitfull. Men have Masques and nets,
But these with wearing will themselves unfold:
They cannot last. No lie grew ever old.
Turne him, and see his Threds: looke, if he be
Friend to himselfe, that would be friend to thee.
For that is first requir'd, A man be his owne.
But he that's too-much that, is friend of none.
Then rest, and a friend's value understand:
It is a richer Purchase than of land.

Ben Jonson (c.1572–1637)

Dear Friends

Dear Friends, reproach me not for what I do,
Nor counsel me, nor pity me; nor say
That I am wearing half my life away
For bubble-work that only fools pursue.
And if my bubbles be too small for you,
Blow bigger then your own: the games we play
To fill the frittered minutes of a day,
Good glasses are to read the spirit through.

And whoso reads may get him some shrewd skill;
And some unprofitable scorn resign,
To praise the very thing that he deplores;
So, friends (dear friends), remember, if you will,
The shame I win for singing is all mine,
The gold I miss for dreaming is all yours.

Edwin Arlington Robinson (1869–1935)

Up-Hill

Does the road wind up-hill all the way?
  Yes, to the very end.
Will the day's journey take the whole long day?
  From morn to night, my friend.

But is there for the night a resting-place?
  A roof for when the slow dark hours begin.
May not the darkness hide it from my face?
  You cannot miss that inn.

Shall I meet other wayfarers at night?
  Those who have gone before.
Then must I knock, or call when just in sight?
  They will not keep you standing at that door.

Shall I find comfort, travel-sore and weak?
  Of labour you shall find the sum.
Will there be beds for me and all who seek?
  Yea, beds for all who come.

Christina Rossetti (1830–1894)

I Dreamed in a Dream

I dream'd in a dream, I saw a city invincible to the
attacks of the whole of the rest of the earth;
I dream'd that was the new City of Friends;
Nothing was greater there than the quality of robust
love – it led the rest;
It was seen every hour in the actions of the men of
that city,
And in all their looks and words.

Walt Whitman (1819–1892)

The Burning of the Leaves

Now is the time for the burning of the leaves.
They go to the fire; the nostril pricks with smoke
Wandering slowly into a weeping mist.
Brittle and blotched, ragged and rotten sheaves!
A flame seizes the smouldering ruin and bites
On stubborn stalks that crackle as they resist.

The last hollyhock's fallen tower is dust;
All the spices of June are a bitter reek,
All the extravagant riches spent and mean.
All burns! The reddest rose is a ghost;
Sparks whirl up, to expire in the mist: the wild
Fingers of fire are making corruption clean.

Now is the time for stripping the spirit bare,
Time for the burning of days ended and done,
Idle solace of things that have gone before:
Rootless hope and fruitless desire are there;
Let them go to the fire, with never a look behind.
The world that was ours is a world that is ours no more.

They will come again, the leaf and the flower, to arise
From squalor of rottenness into the old splendour,
And magical scents to a wondering memory bring;
The same glory, to shine upon different eyes.
Earth cares for her own ruins, naught for ours.
Nothing is certain, only the certain spring.

Laurence Binyon (1869–1943)

Autumn River Song

ON THE BROAD REACH

In the clear green water – the shimmering moon.
In the moonlight – white herons flying.
A young man hears a girl plucking water-chestnuts;
They paddle home together through the night, singing.

Li Po (701–762)
Translated by Florence Ayscough (1878–1942)
and Amy Lowell (1874–1925)

The Sun Used to Shine

The sun used to shine while we two walked
Slowly together, paused and started
Again, and sometimes mused, sometimes talked
As either pleased, and cheerfully parted

Each night. We never disagreed
Which gate to rest on. The to be
And the late past we gave small heed.
We turned from men or poetry

To rumours of the war remote
Only till both stood disinclined
For aught but the yellow flavorous coat
Of an apple wasps had undermined;

Or a sentry of dark betonies,
The stateliest of small flowers on earth,
At the forest verge; or crocuses
Pale purple as if they had their birth

In sunless Hades fields. The war
Came back to mind with the moonrise
Which soldiers in the east afar
Beheld then. Nevertheless, our eyes

Could as well imagine the Crusades
Or Caesar's battles. Everything
To faintness like those rumours fade –
Like the brook's water glittering

Under the moonlight – like those walks
Now – like us two that took them, and
The fallen apples, all the talks
And silence – like memory's sand

When the tide covers it late or soon,
And other men through other flowers
In those fields under the same moon
Go talking and have easy hours.

Edward Thomas (1878–1917)

Love Me Not for Comely Grace

Love not me for comely grace,
  For my pleasing eye or face;
Nor for any outward part,
No, nor for my constant heart:
  For those may fail or turn to ill,
    So thou and I shall sever.
Keep therefore a true woman's eye,
And love me still, but know not why;
  So hast thou the same reason still
    To doat upon me ever!

John Wilbye (1574–1638)

The Tramps

Can you recall, dear comrade, when we tramped God's
 land together,
And we sang the old, old Earth-song, for our youth was
 very sweet;
When we drank and fought and lusted, as we mocked at
 tie and tether,
Along the road to Anywhere, the wide world at our feet.

Along the road to Anywhere, when each day had its story;
When time was yet our vassal, and life's jest was still
 unstale;
When peace unfathomed filled our hearts as, bathed in
 amber glory,
Along the road to Anywhere we watched the sunsets pale.

Alas! the road to Anywhere is pitfalled with disaster;
There's hunger, want, and weariness, yet O we loved it so!
As on we tramped exultantly, and no man was our master,
And no man guessed what dreams were ours, as swinging
 heel and toe,
We tramped the road to Anywhere, the magic road
 to Anywhere,
The tragic road to Anywhere, such dear, dim years ago.

Robert Service (1879–1958)

He Hears With Gladdened Heart the Thunder

He hears with gladdened heart the thunder
  Peal, and loves the falling dew;
He knows the earth above and under –
Sits and is content to view.

He sits beside the dying ember,
  God for hope and man for friend,
Content to see, glad to remember,
  Expectant of the certain end.

Robert Louis Stevenson (1850–1894)

Eternity

FROM *GNOMIC VERSES*

He who binds to himself a Joy
Doth the wingèd life destroy;
But he who kisses the Joy as it flies
Lives in Eternity's sunrise.

William Blake (1757–1827)

The Female Friend

In this imperfect, gloomy scene
  Of complicated ill,
How rarely is a day serene,
  The throbbing bosom still!
Will not a beauteous landscape bright,
  Or music's soothing sound,
Console the heart, afford delight,
  And throw sweet peace around?
They may, but never comfort lend
Like an accomplish'd female friend!

With such a friend, the social hour
  In sweetest pleasure glides;
There is in female charms a power
  Which lastingly abides –
The fragrance of the blushing rose,
  Its tints and splendid hue,
Will with the season decompose,
  And pass as flitting dew;
On firmer ties his joys depend
Who has a polish'd female friend!

The pleasures which from thence arise
  Surpass the blooming flower,
For though it opens to the skies,
  It closes in an hour!
Its sweetness is of transient date,
  Its varied beauties cease –
They can no lasting joys create,
  Impart no lasting peace;
While both arise, and duly blend
In an accomplish'd female friend!

As orbs revolve and years recede,
  As seasons onward roll,
The fancy may on beauties feed,
  With discontented soul!
A thousand objects bright and fair
  May for a moment shine,
Yet many a sigh and many a tear
  But mark their swift decline;
While lasting joys the man attend
Who has a faithful female friend!

Cornelius Whur (1782–1853)

Rendezvous

I count that friendship little worth
  Which has not many things untold,
  Great longings that no words can hold,
And passion-secrets waiting birth.

Along the slender wires of speech
  Some message from the heart is sent;
  But who can tell the whole that's meant?
Our dearest thoughts are out of reach.

I have not seen thee, though mine eyes
    Hold now the image of thy face;
    In vain, through form, I strive to trace
The soul I love: that deeper lies.

A thousand accidents control
    Our meeting here. Clasp hand in hand,
    And swear to meet me in that land
Where friends converse soul to soul.

Henry van Dyke (1852–1933)

Love Lightly Pleased

Let faire or foule my Mistresse be,
Or low, or tall, she pleaseth me;
Or let her walk, or stand, or sit,
The posture hers, I'm pleas'd with it.
Or let her tongue be still, or stir,
Gracefull is ev'ry thing from her.
Or let her Grant, or else Deny,
My Love will fit each Historie.

Robert Herrick (1591–1674)

Real and Imaginary Friends

FROM *THE PICKWICK PAPERS*

Mr Pickwick, having said grace, pauses for an instant, and looks round him. As he does so, the tears roll down his cheeks, in the fulness of his joy.

Let us leave our old friend in one of those moments of unmixed happiness, of which, if we seek them, there are ever some, to cheer our transitory existence here. There are dark shadows on the earth, but its lights are stronger in the contrast. Some men, like bats or owls, have better eyes for the darkness than for the light. We, who have no such optical powers, are better pleased to take our last parting look at the visionary companions of many solitary hours, when the brief sunshine of the world is blazing full upon them.

It is the fate of most men who mingle with the world, and attain even the prime of life, to make many real friends, and lose them in the course of nature. It is the fate of all authors or chroniclers to create imaginary friends, and lose them in the course of art.

Charles Dickens (1812–1870)

Two Friends

The last word this one spoke
was my name. The last word
that one spoke
was my name.

My two friends
had never met. But when they said
that last word
they spoke to each other.

I am proud to have given them a language
of one word. A narrow space
in which, without knowing it,
they met each other at last.

Norman MacCaig (1910–1996)

An Ode On Friendship

VERSE 1

Friendship! peculiar Gift of Heav'n,
  The noble Mind's delight and pride,
To Men and Angels only given,
  To all the lower World deny'd.

Samuel Johnson (1709–1784)

NOVEMBER

A Little Laughter

Our Saviour's Golden Rule

Be you to others kind and true,
As you'd have others be to you;
And neither do nor say to men
Whate'er you would not take again.

Isaac Watts (1674–1748)

A Greeting

(TO W. C.)

But once or twice we met, touched hands.
  To-day between us both expands
  A waste of tumbling waters wide, –
  A waste by me as yet untried,
Vague with the doubt of unknown lands.

Time like a despot speeds his sands:
A year he blots, a day he brands;
  We walked, we talked by Thamis' side
      But once or twice.

What makes a friend? What filmy strands
Are these that turn to iron bands?
  What knot is this so firmly tied
  That naught but Fate can now divide? –
Ah, these are things one understands
      But once or twice!

Austin Dobson (1840–1921)

It Was a Quiet Way

It was a quiet way –
He asked if I was his –
I made no answer of the Tongue
But answer of the Eyes –
And then He bore me on
Before this mortal noise
With swiftness, as of Chariots
And distance, as of Wheels.
This World did drop away
As Acres from the feet
Of one that leaneth from Balloon
Upon an Ether street.
The Gulf behind was not,
The Continents were new –
Eternity it was before
Eternity was due.
No Seasons were to us –
It was not Night nor Morn –
But Sunrise stopped upon the place
And fastened it in Dawn.

Emily Dickinson (1830–1886)

4 NOVEMBER

Friendship

FROM *ESSAYS*

We have a great deal more kindness than is ever spoken. Barring all the selfishness that chills like east winds the world, the whole human family is bathed with an element of love like a fine ether. How many persons we meet in houses, whom we scarcely speak to, whom yet we honor, and who honor us! How many we see in the street, or sit with in church, whom, though silently, we warmly rejoice to be with! Read the language of these wandering eye-beams. The heart knoweth.

Ralph Waldo Emerson (1803–1882)

Constancy Rewarded

I vow'd unvarying faith, and she,
    To whom in full I pay that vow,
Rewards me with variety
    Which men who change can never know.

Coventry Patmore (1823–1896)

A Friend or Two

There's all of pleasure and all of peace
  In a friend or two;
And all your troubles may find release
  Within a friend or two;
It's in the grip of the sleeping hand
On native soil or in alien land,
But the world is made – do you understand –
  Of a friend or two.

A song to sing, and a crust to share
  With a friend or two;
A smile to give and a grief to bear
  With a friend or two;
A road to walk and a goal to win,
An inglenook to find comfort in,
The gladdest hours that we know begin
  With a friend or two.

A little laughter; perhaps some tears
  With a friend or two;
The days, the weeks, and the months and years
  With a friend or two;
A vale to cross and a hill to climb,
A mock at age and a jeer at time –
The prose of life takes the lilt of rhyme
  With a friend or two.

The brother-soul and the brother-heart
  Of a friend or two.
Make us drift on from the crowd apart,
  With a friend or two;
For come days happy or come days sad
We count no hours but the ones made glad
By the hale good times we have ever had
With a friend or two.

Then brim the goblet and quaff the toast
  To a friend or two,
For glad the man who can always boast
  Of a friend or two;
But fairest sight is a friendly face,
The blithest tread is a friendly pace
And heaven will be a better place
  For a friend or two.

Wilbur D. Nesbit (1871–1927)

My Friend

Two days ago with dancing glancing hair,
  With living lips and eyes:
  Now pale, dumb, blind, she lies;
So pale, yet still so fair.

We have not left her yet, not yet alone;
  But soon must leave her where
  She will not miss our care,
Bone of our bone.

Weep not; O friends, we should not weep:
  Our friend of friends lies full of rest;
  No sorrow rankles in her breast,
Fallen fast asleep.

She sleeps below,
  She wakes and laughs above:
  Today, as she walked, let us walk in love;
Tomorrow follow so.

Christina Rossetti (1830–1894)

Companion – North-East Dug-out

He talked of Africa,
　　That fat and easy man.
I'd but to say a word,
　　And straight the tales began.

And when I'd wish to read,
　　That man would not disclose
A thought of harm, but sleep;
　　Hard-breathing through his nose.

Then when I'd wish to hear
　　More tales of Africa,
'Twas but to wake him up,
　　And but a word to say

To press the button, and
　　Keep quiet; nothing more;
For tales of stretching veldt,
　　Kaffir and sullen Boer.

O what a lovely friend!
　　O quiet easy life!
I wonder if his sister
　　Would care to be my wife ...

Ivor Gurney (1890–1937)

To the Author's Wife

Dear Alice, through much mockery of yours
(Impatient of my labours long and slow
And small results that I made haste to show
From time to time), you scornfullest of reviewers,
These verses work'd their way: 'Get on, get on,'
Was mostly my encouragement: But I
Dead to all spurring kept my pace foregone
And long had learnt all laughter to defy.
I thought, moreover, that your laugh (for hard
Would be the portion of the hapless Bard
Who found not in each comment, grave or gay,
Some flattering unction) ... In your laugh, I say
A subtle something glimmer'd; 'twas a laugh,
If half of mockery, yet of pleasure half.
And since, on looking round, I know not who
Will greet my offering with as good a grace
And in their favout give it half a place,
These flights, for fault of better, short and few,
Dear Alice, I must dedicate to you.

Sir Henry Taylor (1800–1886)

Rainbows

If I could catch a rainbow
I would do it just for you.
And share with you its beauty
On the days you're feeling blue.

If I could build a mountain
You could call your very own.
A place to find serenity
A place to be alone.

If I could take your troubles
I would toss them in the sea.
But all these things I'm finding
Are impossible for me,

I cannot build a mountain
Or catch a rainbow fair
But let me be ... what I know best,
A friend that's always there.

Kahlil Gibran (1883–1931)

Sonnet: To Tartar, a Terrier Beauty

Snowdrop of dogs, with ear of brownest dye,
Like the last orphan leaf of naked tree
Which shudders in black autumn; though by thee,
Of hearing careless and untutored eye,
Not understood articulate speech of men
Nor marked the artificial mind of books,
– The mortal's voice eternized by the pen, –
Yet hast thou thought and language all unknown
To Babel's scholars; oft intensest looks,
Long scrutiny over some dark-veined stone
Dost thou bestow, learning dead mysteries
Of the world's birth-day, oft in eager tone
With quick-tailed fellows bandiest prompt replies,
Solicitudes canine, four-footed amities.

Thomas Lovell Beddoes (1803–1849)

The Choice

LINES 74–97

That life may be more comfortable yet,
And all my joys refined, sincere and great,
I'd choose two friends, whose company would be
A great advance to my felicity:
Well-born, of humours suited to my own,
Discreet, and men, as well as books, have known;
Brave, gen'rous, witty, and exactly free
From loose behaviour or formality.
Airy and prudent, merry, but not light;
Quick in discerning, and in judging right.
Secret they should be, faithful to their trust;
In reas'ning cool, strong, temperate and just;
Obliging, open, without huffing, brave,
Brisk in gay talking, and in sober, grave;
Close in dispute, but not tenacious, tried
By solid reason, and let that decide;
Not prone to lust, revenge, or envious hate.
Nor busy meddlers with intrigues of state;
Strangers to slander, and sworn foes to spite:
Not quarrelsome, but stout enough to fight;
Loyal and pious, friends to Caesar, true
As dying martyrs to their Maker too.
In their society, I could not miss
A permanent, sincere, substantial bliss.

John Pomfret (1667–1702)

To an Old Comrade in the Army of Brutus

Dear friend who fought so often, together with me,
In the ranks of Brutus in hardship and in danger,
Under whose sponsorship have you come back,
A citizen again, beneath our sky?

Pompey, we drank together so many times,
And we were together in the Philippi fight,
The day I ran away, leaving my shield,
And Mercury got me out of it, carrying me

In a cloud, in a panic, right through the enemy rage;
But the undertow of a wave carried you back
Into the boiling waters of the war.
Come, stretch your weary legs out under this tree;

Let's dedicate a feast to Jupiter
Just as we told each other we'd do someday.
I've got good food to eat, good wine to drink;
Come celebrate old friendship under the laurel.

Horace (65BC–8BC)
Translated by David Ferry (1924–)

Meat Without Mirth

Eaten I have; and though I had good cheere,
I did not sup, because no friends were there.
Where Mirth and Friends are absent when we Dine
Or Sup, there wants the Incense and the Wine.

Robert Herrick (1591–1674)

XXX

FROM *MORE POEMS*

Shake hands, we shall never be friends, all's over;
  I only vex you the more I try.
All's wrong that ever I've done or said,
And nought to help it in this dull head:
  Shake hands, here's luck, good-bye.

But if you come to a road where danger
  Or guilt or anguish or shame's to share,
Be good to the lad that loves you true
And the soul that was born to die for you,
  And whistle and I'll be there.

A. E. Housman (1859–1936)

The Wish

VERSE 2

Ah, yet, ere I descend to the grave,
May I a small house and large garden have;
And a few friends, and many books, both true,
Both wise, and both delightful too!
    And since love ne'er will from me flee
A Mistress moderately fair,
And good as guardian angels are,
    Only beloved and loving me.

Abraham Cowley (1618–1667)

It's an Owercome Sooth for Age an' Youth

It's an owercome sooth for age an' youth
And it brooks wi' nae denial,
That the dearest friends are the auldest friends
And the young are just on trial.

There's a rival bauld wi' young an' auld
And it's him that has bereft me;
For the surest friends are the auldest friends
And the maist o' mines hae left me.

There are kind hearts still, for friends to fill
And fools to take and break them;
But the nearest friends are the auldest friends
And the grave's the place to seek them.

Robert Louis Stevenson (1850–1894)

One Shelter'd Hare

FROM *THE TASK*, BOOK III, LINES 334–351

Well – one at least is safe. One shelter'd hare
Has never heard the sanguinary yell
Of cruel man, exulting in her woes.
Innocent partner of my peaceful home,
Whom ten long years' experience of my care
Has made at last familiar; she has lost
Much of her vigilant instinctive dread,
Not needful here, beneath a roof like mine.
Yes – thou may'st eat thy bread, and lick the hand
That feeds thee; thou may'st frolic on the floor
At evening, and at night retire secure
To thy straw couch, and slumber unalarm'd.
For I have gain'd thy confidence, have pledg'd
All that is human in me to protect
Thine unsuspecting gratitude and love.
If I survive thee I will dig thy grave;
And when I place thee in it, sighing say,
I knew at least one hare that had a friend.

William Cowper (1731–1800)

The Light of Other Days

Oft, in the stilly night,
    Ere slumber's chain has bound me,
Fond memory brings the light
    Of other days around me;
        The smiles, the tears,
        Of boyhood's years,
    The words of love then spoken;
  The eyes that shone,
  Now dimm'd and gone,
  The cheerful hearts now broken!
Thus, in the stilly night,
      Ere slumber's chain hath bound me,
Sad Memory brings the light
      Of other days around me.

When I remember all
        The friends, so link'd together,
I've seen around me fall,
        Like leaves in wintry weather;
            I feel like one
            Who treads alone
   Some banquet-hall deserted,
            Whose lights are fled,
            Whose garlands dead,
     And all but he departed!
Thus, in the stilly night,
        Ere slumber's chain has bound me,
Sad Memory brings the light
        Of other days around me.

Thomas Moore (1779–1852)

20 NOVEMBER

On the Collar of Tiger

Pray steal me not; I'm Mrs Dingley's,
Whose heart in this four-footed thing lies.

Jonathan Swift (1667–1745)

To a Friend

Go, then, and join the murmuring city's throng!
  Me thou dost leave to solitude and tears;
  To busy phantasies, and boding fears,
Lest ill betide thee; but 't will not be long
Ere the hard season shall be past; till then
  Live happy; sometimes the forsaken shade
  Remembering, and these trees now left to fade;
Nor, mid the busy scenes and hum of men,
Wilt thou my cares forget: in heaviness
  To me the hours shall roll, weary and slow,
  Till mournful autumn past, and all the snow
Of winter pale, the glad hour I shall bless
That shall restore thee from the crowd again,
  To the green hamlet on the peaceful plain.

William Lisle Bowles (1762–1850)

Song

O wert thou in the storm
How I would shield thee:
To keep thee dry and warm
A camp I would build thee.

Though the clouds pour'd again
Not a drop should harm thee,
The music of wind and rain
Rather should charm thee.

O wert thou in a storm
A shed I would build thee;
To keep thee dry and warm,
How I would shield thee.

The rain should not wet thee,
Nor thunder-clap harm thee.
By thy side I would sit me,
To comfort and warm thee.

I would sit by thy side love,
While the dread storm was over
And the wings of an angel
My charmer would cover.

John Clare (1793–1864)

Love's Votary

Others have pleasantness and praise,
        And wealth; and hand and glove
They walk with worship all their days,
        But I have only Love.

And therefore if Love be a fire,
        Then he shall burn me up;
If Love be water out of mire,
        Then I will be the cup.

If Love come worn with wayfaring,
        My breast shall be his bed;
If he come faint and hungering,
        My heart shall be his bread.

If Love delight in vassalage,
        Then I will be his thrall,
Till, when I end my pilgrimage,
        Love give me all for all.

George Augustus Simcox (1841–1905)

Controlling the Tongue

My son, keep well thy tongue, and keep thy friend.
A wicked tongue is worse than a fiend;
My son, from a fiend men may them bless.
My son, God of his endless goodness
Walled a tongue with teeth and lips eke,
For man should him avise what he speak.
My son, full oft, for too much speech
Hath many a man been spilt, as clerkès teach;
But for little speech avisely
Is no man shent, to speak generally.
My son, thy tongue shouldst thou restrain
At all time, but when thou dost thy pain
To speak of God, in honour and prayer.
The first virtue, son, if thou wilt lere,
Is to restrain and keep well thy tongue;
Thus learn children when that they been young.
My son, of muckle speaking evil-avised,
Where less speaking had enough sufficed,
Cometh muckle harm; thus was me told and taught.
In muckle speech sin wanteth nought.
Wost thou whereof a rakel tongue serveth?
Right as a sword forcutteth and forcarveth
An arm a-two, my dear son, right so
A tongue cutteth friendship all a-two.

Geoffrey Chaucer (c.1343–1400)

25 NOVEMBER

A Sister

FROM *GOBLIN MARKET*, LINES 652–567

For there is no friend like a sister
In calm or stormy weather;
To cheer one on the tedious way,
To fetch one if one goes astray,
To lift one if one totters down,
To strengthen whilst one stands.

Christina Rossetti (1830–1894)

Sonnet XXX

When to the sessions of sweet silent thought
I summon up remembrance of things past,
I sigh the lack of many a thing I sought,
And with old woes new wail my dear time's waste:
Then can I drown an eye, unused to flow,
For precious friends hid in death's dateless night,
And weep afresh love's long since canceled woe,
And moan th' expense of many a vanished sight;
Then can I grieve at grievances foregone,
And heavily from woe to woe tell o'er
The sad account of fore-bemoanèd moan,
Which I new pay as if not paid before.
    But if the while I think on thee, dear friend,
    All losses are restor'd, and sorrows end.

William Shakespeare (1564–1616)

Sonnet III

At nine years old I was Love's willing Page:
Poets love earlier than other men,
And would love later, but for the prodigal pen.
'Oh! wherefore hast thou, Love, ceased now to engage
Thy servitor, found true in every stage
Of all eleven Springs gone by since then?'
Vain quest! – and I, No more Love's denizen,
Sought the pure leisure of the Golden Age.
But lately wandering from the world apart,
Chance brought me where, before her quiet nest,
A village-girl was standing without art.
My soul sprang up from its lethargic rest,
The slack veins tightened all across my heart,
And love was once more aching in my breast.

Coventry Patmore (1823–1896)

The Friends

I had some friends – but I dreamed that they were dead –
Who used to dance with lanterns round a little boy in bed;
Green and white lanterns that waved to and fro:
But I haven't seen a Firefly since ever so long ago!

I had some friends – their crowns were in the sky –
Who used to nod and whisper when a little boy went by,
As the nuts began to tumble and the breeze began to blow:
And I haven't seen a Cocoa-palm since ever so long ago!

I had a friend – he came up from Cape Horn,
With a Coal-sack on his shoulder when a little boy
  was born.
He heard me learn to talk, and he helped me thrive
  and grow:
But I haven't seen the Southern Cross since ever so
  long ago!

I had a boat – I out and let her drive,
Till I found my dream was foolish, for my friends were
  all alive.
The Cocoa-palms were real, and the Southern Cross
  was true:
And the Fireflies were dancing – so I danced too!

Rudyard Kipling (1865–1936)

Thanksgiving

For flowers that bloom about our feet;
For tender grass so fresh, so sweet;
For the song of bird and hum of bee;
For all things fair we hear or see,
Father in heaven, we thank Thee.

For blue of stream and blue of sky;
For pleasant shade of branches high;
For fragrant air and cooling breeze;
For beauty of the blooming trees,
Father in heaven, we thank Thee.

Ralph Waldo Emerson (1803–1882)

The Shortest and Sweetest of Songs

Come
Home.

George MacDonald (1824–1905)

DECEMBER

Winter is Deck'd with a Smile

Natural History

(A LETTER TO KATHERINE, FROM THE
KING EDWARD HOTEL, TORONTO)

The spider, dropping down from twig,
Unfolds a plan of her devising,
A thin premeditated rig
To use in rising.

And all that journey down through space,
In cool descent, and loyal hearted,
She spins a ladder to the place
From where she started.

Thus I, gone forth, as spiders do,
In spider's web a truth discerning,
Attach one silken thread to you
For my returning.

E. B. White (1899–1985)

'How Pleasant to Know Mr. Lear!'

'How pleasant to know Mr. Lear!'
  Who has written such volumes of stuff!
Some think him ill-tempered and queer,
  But a few find him pleasant enough.

His mind is concrete and fastidious; –
  His nose is remarkably big; –
His visage is more or less hideous; –
  His beard it resembles a wig.

He has ears, and two eyes, and ten fingers, –
  (Leastways if you reckon two thumbs;)
Long ago he was one of the singers,
  But now he is one of the dumms.

He sits in a beautiful parlour,
  With hundreds of books on the wall;
He drinks a great deal of Marsala,
  But never gets tipsy at all.

He has many friends, laymen and clerical;
  Old Foss is the name of his cat;
His body is perfectly spherical; –
  He weareth a runcible hat.

When he walks in waterproof white
  The children run after him so!
Calling out, – 'He's gone out in his night-
  gown, that crazy old Englishman, – O'

He weeps by the side of the ocean,
  He weeps on the top of the hill;
He purchases pancakes and lotion,
  And chocolate shrimps from the mill.

He reads, but he cannot speak, Spanish;
  He cannot abide ginger beer. –
Ere the days of his pilgrimage vanish, –
  'How pleasant to know Mr. Lear!'

Edward Lear (1812–1888)

Love and Friendship

Love is like the wild rose briar,
Friendship, like the holly tree
The holly is dark when the rose briar blooms
But which will bloom most constantly?

The wild rose briar is sweet in spring,
Its summer blossoms scent the air;
Yet wait till winter comes again
And who will call the wild-briar fair?

Then scorn the silly rose-wreath now
And deck thee with the holly's sheen,
That when December blights thy brow
He still may leave thy garland green.

Emily Brontë (1818–1848)

To a Cat

I

Stately, kindly, lordly friend,
    Condescend
Here to sit by me, and turn
Glorious eyes that smile and burn,
Golden eyes, love's lustrous meed,
On the golden page I read.

All your wondrous wealth of hair,
    Dark and fair,
Silken-shaggy, soft and bright
As the clouds and beams of night,
Pays my reverent hand's caress
Back with friendlier gentleness.

Dogs may fawn on all and some
    As they come;
You, a friend of loftier mind,
Answer friends alone in kind.
Just your foot upon my hand
Softly bids it understand.

Morning round this silent sweet
    Garden-seat
Sheds its wealth of gathering light,
Thrills the gradual clouds with might,
Changes woodland, orchard, heath,
Lawn, and garden there beneath.

Fair and dim they gleamed below:
    Now they glow
Deep as even your sunbright eyes,
Fair as even the wakening skies.
Can it not or can it be
Now that you give thanks to see?

May not you rejoice as I,
    Seeing the sky
Change to heaven revealed, and bid
Earth reveal the heaven it hid
All night long from stars and moon,
Now the sun sets all in tune?

What within you wakes with day
    Who can say?
All too little may we tell,
Friends who like each other well,
What might haply, if we might,
Bid us read our lives aright.

II

Wild on woodland ways your sires
    Flashed like fires:
Fair as flame and fierce and fleet
As with wings on wingless feet
Shone and sprang your mother, free,
Bright and brave as wind or sea.

Free and proud and glad as they,
  Here to-day
Rests or roams their radiant child,
Vanquished not, but reconciled,
Free from curb of aught above
Save the lovely curb of love.

Love through dreams of souls divine
    Fain would shine
Round a dawn whose light and song
Then should right our mutual wrong –
Speak, and seal the love-lit law
Sweet Assisi's seer foresaw.

Dreams were theirs; yet haply may
    Dawn a day
When such friends and fellows born,
Seeing our earth as fair at morn,
May for wiser love's sake see
More of heaven's deep heart than we.

Algernon Charles Swinburne (1837–1909)

Cyril and Florian

FROM *THE PRINCESS*, PART I

That morning in the presence room I stood
With Cyril and with Florian, my two friends:
The first, a gentleman of broken means
(His father's fault) but given to starts and bursts
Of revel; and the last, my other heart,
And almost my half-self, for still we moved
Together, twinn'd as horse's ear and eye.

Alfred, Lord Tennyson (1809–1892)

To My Dear and Loving Husband

If ever two were one, then surely we.
If ever man were loved by wife, then thee.
If ever wife was happy in a man,
Compare with me, ye women, if you can.
I prize thy love more than whole mines of gold,
Or all the riches that the East doth hold.
My love is such that rivers cannot quench,
Nor ought but love from thee give recompense.
Thy love is such I can no way repay;
The heavens reward thee manifold, I pray.
Then while we live, in love let's so persevere,
That when we live no more, we may live ever.

Anne Bradstreet (c.1612–1672)

Portrait of a Lady

THOU HAST COMMITTED –
FORNICATION: BUT THAT WAS IN ANOTHER COUNTRY,
AND BESIDES, THE WENCH IS DEAD.

THE JEW OF MALTA, PART 1

I

Among the smoke and fog of a December afternoon
You have the scene arrange itself – as it will seem to do –
With 'I have saved this afternoon for you';
And four wax candles in the darkened room,
Four rings of light upon the ceiling overhead,
An atmosphere of Juliet's tomb
Prepared for all the things to be said, or left unsaid.
We have been, let us say, to hear the latest Pole
Transmit the Preludes, through his hair and finger-tips.
'So intimate, this Chopin, that I think his soul
Should be resurrected only among friends
Some two or three, who will not touch the bloom
That is rubbed and questioned in the concert room.'
– And so the conversation slips
Among velleities and carefully caught regrets
Through attenuated tones of violins
Mingled with remote cornets
And begins.

'You do not know how much they mean to me, my friends,
And how, how rare and strange it is, to find
In a life composed so much, so much of odds and ends,
(For indeed I do not love it ... you knew? you are not blind!

How keen you are!)
To find a friend who has these qualities,
Who has, and gives
Those qualities upon which friendship lives.
How much it means that I say this to you –
Without these friendships – life, what *cauchemar*!'

Among the winding of the violins
And the ariettes
Of cracked cornets
Inside my brain a dull tom-tom begins
Absurdly hammering a prelude of its own,
Capricious monotone
That is at least one definite 'false note.'
– Let us take the air, in a tobacco trance,
Admire the monuments,
Discuss the late events,
Correct our watches by the public clocks.
Then sit for half an hour and drink our bocks.

T. S. Eliot (1888–1965)

Sonnet LXXVI

Why is my verse so barren of new pride,
So far from variation or quick change?
Why with the time do I not glance aside
To new-found methods and to compounds strange?
Why write I still all one, ever the same,
And keep invention in a noted weed,
That every word doth almost tell my name,
Showing their birth, and where they did proceed?
O know, sweet love, I always write of you,
And you and love are still my argument,
So all my best is dressing old words new,
Spending again what is already spent:
For as the sun is daily new and old,
So is my love still telling what is told.

William Shakespeare (1564–1616)

An Invite to Eternity

Wilt thou go with me sweet maid
Say maiden wilt thou go with me
Through the valley-depths of shade
Of night and dark obscurity
Where the path has lost its way
Where the sun forgets the day
Where there's nor life nor light to see
Sweet maiden, wilt thou go with me

Where stones will turn to flooding streams
Where plains will rise like ocean-waves
Where life will fade like visioned dreams
And mountains darken into caves
Say maiden wilt thou go with me
Through this sad non-identity
Where parents live and are forgot
And sisters live and know us not

Say maiden wilt thou go with me
In this strange death of life-to-be
To live in death and be the same
Without this life or home or name
At once to be and not to be
That was and is not – yet to see
Things pass like shadows and the sky
Above, below, around us lie.

The land of shadows wilt thou trace
And look nor know each other's face
The present mixed with seasons gone
And past and present all as one
Say maiden can thy life be led
To join the living with the dead
The trace thy footsteps on with me
We're wed to one eternity.

John Clare (1793–1864)

New Friends and Old Friends

Make new friends, but keep the old;
Those are silver, these are gold.
New-made friendships, like new wine,
Age will mellow and refine.
Friendships that have stood the test –
Time and change – are surely best;
Brow may wrinkle, hair grow gray,
Friendship never knows decay.
For 'mid old friends, tried and true,
Once more we our youth renew.
But old friends, alas! may die,
New friends must their place supply.
Cherish friendship in your breast –
New is good, but old is best;
Make new friends, but keep the old;
Those are silver, these are gold.

Joseph Parry (1841–1903)

XXI

BREDON HILL
FROM *A SHROPSHIRE LAD*

In summertime on Bredon
  The bells they sound so clear;
Round both the shires they ring them
  In steeples far and near,
  A happy noise to hear.

Here of a Sunday morning
  My love and I would lie,
And see the coloured counties,
  And hear the larks so high
  About us in the sky.

The bells would ring to call her
  In valleys miles away;
'Come all to church, good people;
  Good people come and pray.'
  But here my love would stay.

And I would turn and answer
  Among the springing thyme,
'Oh, peal upon our wedding,
  And we will hear the chime,
  And come to church in time.'

But when the snows at Christmas
  On Bredon top were strown,
My love rose up so early
  And stole out unbeknown
  And went to church alone.

They tolled the one bell only,
  Groom there was none to see,
The mourners followed after,
  And so to church went she,
  And would not wait for me.

The bells they sound on Bredon,
  And still the steeples hum,
'Come all to church, good people,' –
  Oh, noisy bells, be dumb;
  I hear you, I will come.

A. E. Housman (1859–1936)

The Winter Nosegay

What nature, alas! has denied
  To the delicate growth of our isle,
Art has in a measure supplied,
  And winter is deck'd with a smile.
See, Mary, what beauties I bring
  From the shelter of that sunny shed,
Where the flow'rs have the charms of the spring,
  Though abroad they are frozen and dead.

'Tis a bow'r of Arcadian sweets,
  Where Flora is still in her prime,
A fortress to which she retreats,
  From the cruel assaults of the clime.
While earth wears a mantle of snow,
  These pinks are as fresh and as gay,
As the fairest and sweetest that blow,
  On the beautiful bosom of May.

See how they have safely surviv'd
  The frowns of a sky so severe;
Such Mary's true love that has liv'd
  Through many a turbulent year.
The charms of the late blowing rose
  Seem grac'd with a livelier hue,
And the winter of sorrow best shows
  The truth of a friend, such as you.

William Cowper (1731–1800)

Outwitted

He drew a circle that shut me out –
Heretic, rebel, a thing to flout.
But Love and I had the wit to win:
We drew a circle that took him in!

Edwin Markham (1852–1940)

Any Wife or Husband

Let us be guests in one another's house
With deferential 'No' and courteous 'Yes';
Let us take care to hide our foolish moods
Behind a certain show of cheerfulness.

Let us avoid all sullen silences;
We should find fresh and sprightly things to say;
I must be fearful lest you find me dull,
And you must dread to bore me any way.

Let us knock gently at each other's heart,
Glad of a chance to look within – and yet
Let us remember that to force one's way
Is the unpardoned breach of etiquette.

So shall I be hostess – you, the host –
Until all need for entertainment ends;
We shall be lovers when the last door shuts,
But what is better still – we shall be friends.

Carol Haynes (1897–?)

A Dumb Friend

I planted a young tree when I was young;
  But now the tree is grown and I am old:
  There wintry robin shelters from the cold
    And tunes his silver tongue.

A green and living tree I planted it,
  A glossy-foliaged tree of evergreen:
  All thro' the noontide heat it spread a screen
    Whereunder I might sit.

But now I only watch it where it towers:
  I, sitting at my window, watch it tossed
  By rattling gale, or silvered by the frost;
    Or, when sweet summer flowers,

Wagging its round green head with stately grace
  In tender winds that kiss it and go by:
  It shows a green full age; and what show I?
    A faded wrinkled face.

So often have I watched it, till mine eyes
  Have filled with tears and I have ceased to see;
  That now it seems a very friend to me
    In all my secrets wise.

A faithful pleasant friend, who year by year
  Grew with my growth and strengthened with my strength,
  But whose green lifetime shows a longer length:
    When I shall not sit here

It still will bud in spring, and shed rare leaves
  In autumn, and in summer heat give shade,
  And warmth in winter; when my bed is made
    In shade the cypress weaves.

Christina Rossetti (1830–1894)

If I Had Known

If I had known what trouble you were bearing;
What griefs were in the silence of your face;
I would have been more gentle and more caring,
And tried to give you gladness for a space.
I would have brought more warmth into the place,
  If I had known.

If I had known what thoughts despairing drew you;
(Why do we never try to understand?)
I would have lent a little friendship to you,
And slipped my hand within your hand,
And made your stay more pleasant in the land,
  If I had known.

Mary Carolyn Davies (1888–?)

The Life That I Have

The life that I have
Is all that I have
And the life that I have
Is yours.

The love that I have
Of the life that I have
Is yours and yours and yours.

A sleep I shall have
A rest I shall have
Yet death will be but a pause.

For the peace of my years
In the long green grass
Will be yours and yours and yours.

Leo Marks (1920–2001)

A Friend's Greeting

I'd like to be the sort of friend that you have been to me;
I'd like to be the help that you've been always glad to be;
I'd like to mean as much to you each minute of the day
As you have meant, old friend of mine, to me along
  the way.

I'd like to do the big things and the splendid things for you,
To brush the gray from out your skies and leave them
  only blue;
I'd like to say the kindly things that I so oft have heard,
And feel that I could rouse your soul the way that mine
  you've stirred.

I'd like to give you back the joy that you have given me,
Yet that were wishing you a need I hope will never be;
I'd like to make you feel as rich as I, who travel on
Undaunted in the darkest hours with you to lean upon.

I'm wishing at this Christmas time that I could but repay
A portion of the gladness that you've strewn along my way;
And could I have one wish this year, this only would it be:
I'd like to be the sort of friend that you have been to me.

Edgar Guest (1881–1959)

Friendship of Young Poets

There must have been more than just one of us
But we never met. Each kept in his world of loss
The promise of literary days, the friendship
Of poets, mysterious, that sharing of the books
And talking in whispers in crowded bars
Suspicious enough to be taken for love.

We never met. My youth was as private
As the bank at midnight, and in its safety
No talking behind backs, no one alike enough
To be pretentious with and quote lines at.

There is a boat on the river now, and
Two young men, one rowing, one reading aloud.
The shirt sleeves fill with the wind, and from the oars
Drop scales of perfect river like melting glass.

Douglas Dunn (1942–)

To His Friend to Avoid Contention of Words

Words beget Anger: Anger brings forth blowes;
Blows make of dearest friends immortall Foes.
For which prevention (Sociate) let there be
Betwixt us two no more *Logomachie.*
Farre better 'twere for either to be mute,
Than for to murder friendship, by dispute.

Robert Herrick (1591–1674)

In an Artist's Studio

One face looks out from all his canvases,
        One selfsame figure sits or walks or leans;
        We found her hidden just behind those screens,
That mirror gave back all her loveliness.
A queen in opal or in ruby dress,
        A nameless girl in freshest summer-greens,
    A saint, an angel – every canvas means
The same one meaning, neither more nor less.
He feeds upon her face by day and night,
        And she with true kind eyes looks back on him
Fair as the moon and joyful as the light:
        Not wan with waiting, not with sorrow dim;
Not as she is, but was when hope shone bright;
        Not as she is, but as she fills his dream.

Christina Rossetti (1830–1894)

These Verses Were Made by Michaell Drayton Esquier Poett Lawreatt the Night Before Hee Dyed

Soe well I love thee, as without thee I
Love Nothing, yf I might Chuse, I'de rather dye
Than bee one day debarde thy companye

Since Beasts, and plantes doe growe, and live and move
Beastes are those men, that such a life appròve:
Hee onlye Lives, that Deadly is in Love

The Corne that in the grownd is sowen first dies
And of one seed doe manye Eares arise
Love, this worldes Corne, by dying Multiplies

The seeds of Love first by thy eyes weare throwne
Into a grownd untild, a hearte unknowne
To beare such fruitt, tyll by thy handes t'was sowen

Looke as your Looking glass by Chance may fall
Devyde and breake in manye peyces smale
And yett shewes forth, the selfe same face in all

Proportions, Features Graces just the same,
And in the smalest peyce as well the name
Of Fayrest one deserves, as in the richest frame

Soe all my Thoughts are peyces but of you
Whiche put together makes a Glass soe true
As I therein noe others face but yours can Viewe

Michael Drayton (1563–1631)

23 DECEMBER

Nature Assigns the Sun

Nature assigns the Sun –
That – is Astronomy –
Nature cannot enact a Friend –
That – is Astrology.

Emily Dickinson (1830–1886)

The Meeting

After so long an absence
    At last we meet again:
Does the meeting give us pleasure,
    Or does it give us pain?

The tree of life has been shaken,
    And but few of us linger now,
Like the Prophet's two or three berries
    In the top of the uppermost bough.

We cordially greet each other
    In the old, familiar tone;
And we think, though we do not say it,
    How old and gray he is grown!

We speak of a Merry Christmas
    And many a Happy New Year;
But each in his heart is thinking
    Of those that are not here.

We speak of friends and their fortunes,
    And of what they did and said,
Till the dead alone seem living,
    And the living alone seem dead.

And at last we hardly distinguish
    Between the ghosts and the guests;
And a mist and shadow of sadness
    Steals over our merriest jests.

Henry Wadsworth Longfellow (1807–1882)

He Wishes for the Cloths of Heaven

Had I the heavens' embroidered cloths,
Enwrought with golden and silver light,
The blue and the dim and the dark cloths
Of night and light and the half-light,
I would spread the cloths under your feet:
But I, being poor, have only my dreams;
I have spread my dreams under your feet;
Tread softly because you tread on my dreams.

W. B. Yeats (1865–1939)

Skating in the Evening

FROM *THE PRELUDE*

And in the frosty season, when the sun
Was set, and visible for many a mile
The cottage windows blazed through the twilight gloom,
I heeded not their summons: happy time
It was indeed for all of us – for me
It was a time of rapture! Clear and loud
The village clock tolled six, – I wheeled about,
Proud and exalting like an untired horse
That cares not for his home. All shod with steel.
We hissed along the polished ice in games
Confederate, imitative of the chase
And woodland pleasures, – the resounding horn,
The pack loud chiming, and the hunted hare.
So through the darkness and the cold we flew,
And not a voice was idle; with the din
Smitten, the precipices rang aloud;
The leafless trees and every icy crag
Tinkled like iron; while far distant hills
Into the tumult sent an alien sound
Of melancholy not unnoticed, while the stars
Eastward were sparkling clear, and in the west
The orange sky of evening died away.
Not seldom from the uproar I retired
Into a silent bay, or sportively
Glanced sideway, leaving the tumultuous throng,
To cut across the reflex of a star

That fled, and, flying still before me, gleamed
Upon the glassy plain; and oftentimes,
When we had given our bodies to the wind,
And all the shadowy banks on either side
Came sweeping through the darkness, spinning still
The rapid line of motion, then at once
Have I, reclining back upon my heels,
Stopped short; yet still the solitary cliffs
Wheeled by me – even as if the earth had rolled
With visible motion her diurnal round!
Behind me they did stretch in solemn train,
Feebler and feebler, and I stood and watched
Till all was tranquil as in a dreamless sleep.

William Wordsworth (1770–1850)

The Manifold Use of Friendship

FROM *ON FRIENDSHIP*

The best way to represent to life the manifold use of friendship, is to cast and see how many things there are which a man cannot do himself; and then it will appear that it was a sparing speech of the ancients, to say, that 'a friend is another himself'; for that a friend is far more than himself. Men have their time, and die many times, in desire of some things which they principally take to heart; the bestowing of a child, the finishing of a work, or the like. If a man have a true friend, he may rest almost secure that the care of those things will continue after him. So that a man hath, as it were, two lives in his desires. A man hath a body, and that body is confined to a place; but where friendship is, all offices of life are as it were granted to him and his deputy. For he may exercise them by his friend. How many things are there which a man cannot, with any face or comeliness, say or do himself? A man can scarce allege his own merits with modesty, much less extol them; a man cannot sometimes brook to supplicate or beg; and a number of the like. But all these things are graceful, in a friend's mouth, which are blushing in a man's own. So again, a man's person hath many proper relations which he cannot put off. A man cannot speak to his son but as a father; to his wife but as a husband; to his enemy but upon terms: whereas a friend may speak as the case requires, and not as it sorteth with the person. But to enumerate these things were endless; I have given the rule, where a man cannot fitly play his own part; if he have not a friend, he may quit the stage.

Francis Bacon (1561–1626)

IV

FROM *ADDITIONAL POEMS*

It is no gift I tender,
  A loan is all I can;
But do not scorn the lender;
  Man gets no more from man.

Oh, mortal man may borrow
  What mortal man can lend;
And 'twill not end to-morrow,
  Though sure enough 'twill end.

If death and time are stronger,
  A love may yet be strong;
The world will last for longer,
  But this will last for long.

A. E. Housman (1859–1936)

The Cat that Walked by Himself

Pussy can sit by the fire and sing,
  Pussy can climb a tree,
Or play with a silly old cork and string
  To 'muse herself, not me.
But I like *Binkie* my dog, because
  He knows how to behave;
So, *Binkie's* the same as the First Friend was,
  And I am the Man in the Cave!

Pussy will play Man-Friday till
  It's time to wet her paw
And make her walk on the window-sill
  (For the footprint Crusoe saw);
Then she fluffles her tail and mews,
  And scratches and won't attend.
But *Binkie* will play whatever I choose,
  And he is my true First Friend!

Pussy will rub my knees with her head
  Pretending she loves me hard;
But the very minute I go to my bed
  Pussy runs out in the yard,
And there she stays till the morning-light;
  So I know it is only pretend;
But *Binkie*, he snores at my feet all night,
  And he is my Firstest Friend!

Rudyard Kipling (1865–1936)

We Have Lived and Loved Together

We have lived and loved together
  Through many changing years;
We have shared each other's gladness
  And wept each other's tears;
I have known ne'er a sorrow
  That was long unsoothed by thee;
For thy smiles can make a summer
  Where darkness else would be.

Like the leaves that fall around us
  In autumn's fading hours,
Are the traitor's smiles, that darken
  When the cloud of sorrow lowers;
And through many such we've known, love,
  Too prone, alas, to range,
We both can speak of one love
  Which time can never change.

We have lived and loved together
  Through many changing years,
We have shared each other's gladness
  And wept each other's tears.
And let us hope the future,
  As the past has been will be:
I will share with thee my sorrows,
  And thou thy joys with me.

Charles Jefferys (1807–1865)

Auld Lang Syne

Should auld acquaintance be forgot,
  And never brought to min'?
Should auld acquaintance be forgot,
  And auld lang syne?

For auld lang syne, my dear,
  For auld lang syne.
We'll tak a cup o' kindness yet,
  For auld lang syne.

We twa hae run about the braes,
  And po'd the gowans fine;
But we've wander'd mony a weary fit,
  Sin' auld lang syne.

We twa hae paidled i' the burn,
  Frae morning sun till dine;
But seas between us braid hae roar'd
  Sin' auld lang syne.

And there's a hand, my trusty fiere,
  And gie's a hand o' thine;
And we'll tak a right guid-willie waught,
  For auld lang syne.

And surely ye'll be your pint stowp,
  And surely I'll be mine,
And we'll tak a cup o' kindness yet,
  For auld lang syne.

Robert Burns (1759–1796)

Traditional Gaelic Blessing

May the road rise up to meet you.
May the wind be always at your back.
May the sun shine warm upon your face,
And rains fall soft upon your fields.
And until we meet again,
May God hold you in the palm of his hand.

Anon

Index of first lines

A friend once won need never be lost, if we will be only trusty and true ourselves 40
A little health 29
A principal fruit of friendship 55
A ruddy drop of manly blood 332
'A Temple to Friendship;' said Laura, enchanted 192
Abou Ben Adhem (may his tribe increase!) 35
After so long an absence 468
Ah *Ben*! 114
Ah, yet, ere I descend to the grave 420
All day long I have been working 163–4
All paths lead to you 320
Among all lovely things my Love had been 249
Among the smoke and fog of a December afternoon 447–8
And a youth said, Speak to us of Friendship 375–6
And have we done with War at last? 278
And in the frosty season, when the sun 470–1
And see where surly Winter passes off 86
As I walked out one evening 330
As late I rambled in the happy fields 238
As Lawrell leaves that cease not to be grene 147
As one who, walking in the twilight gloom 326–7
Ask nothing more of me, sweet 16
At lunchtime I bought a huge orange – 104
At nine years old I was Love's willing Page 432
At the mid hour of night, when stars are weeping, I fly 216

Bailey Bowling, McLean cuts him late for one 247
Be you to others kind and true 404
Beauty and love are all my dream 308
Beauty is but composure, and we find 377
Because I liked you better 170
Before the Roman came to Rye or out to Severn strode 251–2
Being her friend, I do not care, not I 355
Best and brightest, come away 77–9
Bright star, would I were stedfast as thou art – 30
But once or twice we met, touched hands 405

Can we forget one friend 151
Can you recall, dear comrade, when we tramped God's land together 392
Choose judiciously thy friends; for to discard them is undesirable 146
Come 435
Come, be my Valentine 64
Come, dear old comrade, you and I 61–3
Come down, O maid, from yonder mountain height 177–8
Come, let us now resolve at last 18
Come live with me and be my love 181–2
Come, sweetheart, listen, for I have a thing 81
Come when the nights are bright with stars 21

Dear Alice, through much mockery of yours 413
Dear friend who fought so often, together with me 417
Dear Friends, reproach me not for what I do 384
Does the road wind up-hill all the way 385
Doors, where my heart was used to beat 57

Eaten I have; and though I had good cheere 418
Eph. What Friendship is, Ardelia show 273
Even the rainbow has a body 264

False though she be to me and Love 39
Fast falls the snow, O lady mine 71
Fidelity and love are two different things, like a flower and a gem 293–4
For flowers that bloom about our feet 434
For friendship is a partnership, and as a man is to himself 197
For her gait, if she be walking 360
For I will consider my Cat Jeoffry 349–50
For there is no friend like a sister 430
For thus the royal mandate ran 140
For when two soules are chang'd and mixed soe 54
Forsake not an old friend 284
Frail the white rose, and frail are 226
Friend of mine! whose lot was cast 165–6
Friend of my many years 129

Friends, not adopted with a school-boy's haste 98
Friendship is no plant of hasty growth 105
Friendship (like Heraldry) is hereby known 288
Friendship maketh indeed a fair day in the affections 245
Friendship needs no studied phrases 76
Friendship! peculiar Gift of Heav'n 401
From Brooklyn, over the Brooklyn Bridge, on this fine morning 172–4

Geniuses of countless nations 361
Go lovely Rose 223
Go, then, and join the murmuring city's throng! 426
Good-bye! a kind good-bye 102

Had I the heavens' embroidered cloths 469
Harken that happy shout – the school-house door 242
He drew a circle that shut me out – 456
He hears with gladdened heart the thunder 393
He meets, by heavenly chance express 159
He talked of Africa 412
He who binds to himself a Joy 394
Health is the first good lent to men 42
Heaven runs over 34
Here's health to those that I love 263
His friends he loved. His direst earthly foes – 266
'Hope' is the thing with feathers – 51
How do I love thee? Let me count the ways 371
How happy uncle us'd to be 253–4
How many gifted pens have penned 176
'How pleasant to know Mr. Lear!' 439–40
How sweet is the Shepherd's sweet lot! 131

I am in love, meantime, you think; no doubt you would think so 38
I and Pangur Bán my cat 110–11
I ask but one thing of you, only one 228
I cannot choose but think upon the time 14
I cannot promise you a life of sunshine 158
I count that friendship little worth 397
I dare not ask to kisse 267
I did not live until this time 153–4

I dream'd in a dream, I saw a city invincible to the 386
I dwell in Grace's court 32–3
I envy not in any moods 342
I had some friends – but I dreamed that they were dead – 433
I have a kindly neighbor, one who stands 372
I have examin'd and do find 333–4
I heard a linnet courting 135–6
I hid my love when young while I 250
I know the thing that's most uncommon 130
I live in you, you live in me 340
I met Louisa in the shade 180
I ne'er was struck before that hour 329
I ne'r was drest in Forms; nor can I bend 96–7
I planted a young tree when I was young 458–9
I played with you 'mid cowslips blowing 220–2
I saw him pass as the new day dawned 206
'I saw you take his kiss!' ' 'Tis true.' 382
I shot an arrow into the air 133
I thank all who have loved me in their hearts 75
I thank you, kind and best beloved friend 356
I think awhile of Love, and while I think 344–6
I think of thee! – my thoughts do twine & bud 171
I vow'd unvarying faith, and she 408
I went by footpath and by stile 237
I wish I could remember that first day 359
I'd like to be the sort of friend that you have been to me 462
If ever I saw blessing in the air 132
If ever two were one, then surely we 446
If from my lips some angry accents fell 50
If I can stop one Heart from breaking 44
If I could catch a rainbow 414
If I had but a friend! Why, I have three 108
If I had known what trouble you were bearing 460
If no one ever marries me – 19
If thou must love me, let it be for nought 17
If truth in hearts that perish 373
If you were coming in the Fall 362
I'll range around the shady bowers 243–4
I'm Nobody! Who are you? 229

I'm thankful that my life doth not deceive 315
In summertime on Bredon 453–4
In the clear green water – the shimmering moon 388
In this imperfect, gloomy scene 395–6
Is it the wind of the dawn that I hear in the pine overhead? 208
Is love so prone to change and rot 157
It is a sweet thing, friendship, a dear balm 12
It is no gift I tender 473
It is not growing like a tree 167
It is not what we say or sing 298–300
It is the first mild day of March: 112–13
It is the pride of Arete to grace 103
It lies not in our power to love or hate 374
It was a quiet way – 406
It was not in the winter 255
It's an owercome sooth for age an' youth 421

Jacke and *Jone*, they think no ill 290–1
Jenny kissed me when we met 194

laura raises the empty teacup to my lips 115
Lavinia: 352
Let faire or foule my Mistresse be 398
Let me but live my life from year to year 88
Let me go where'er I will 65
Let me not to the marriage of true minds 49
Let us be guests in one another's house 457
Let us go into the fields love and see the green tree 230–1
'Let us not speak, for the love we bear one another – 58
Let us walk where reeds are growing 256
Light, so low upon earth 366
Like thee I once have stemm'd the sea of life 199
Lonely, save for a few faint stars, the sky 219
Love and the gentle heart are one same thing 56
Love drowsy days and stormy nights 193
Love is a circle that doth restlesse move 67
Love is like the wild rose briar 441
Love is not all: it is not meat or drink 37
Love lives beyond 149–50
Love meet me in the green glen 205

Love not me for comely grace 391
Love without hope, as when the young bird-catcher 287
Loving friend, the gift of one 137–9
Luckes, my faire falcon, and your fellowes all 28

Make new friends, but keep the old 452
Martial, the things that do attain 358
Mary had a little lamb 142
May the road rise up to meet you 477
May we, then, never know each other 271
Moreover, how great the power of friendship is 234
Mr Pickwick, having said grace, pauses for an instant 399
My boat is on the shore 280–1
My friend, my bonny friend, when we are old 90
My heart is like a singing bird 331
My luve is like a red, red rose 236
My son, keep well thy tongue, and keep thy friend 429
My true love hath my hart, and I have his 246

Nature assigns the Sun – 467
No image carved with coonnying hand, no cloth of purple dye 60
No labor-saving machine 80
Nothing is so beautiful as Spring – 168
Now is the time for the burning of the leaves 387
Now must I these three praise – 369–70
Now the Spring is waking 109

O friend beloved, whose curious skill 15
O, one I need to love me 89
O sigh no more, love, sigh no more 45
O sweet delight, O more then humane blisse 322
O wert thou in the storm 427
O who will walk a mile with me 279
Of all the heavenly giftes, that mortall men commend 239
Of that short Roll of friends writ in my heart 22
Oft, in the stilly night 423–4
Oh, the comfort – the inexpressible comfort of 99
Old Fitz, who from your suburb grange 353–4
Old friends are best! And so to you 100
on the fifth floor in montmartre 145

One day I wrote her name upon the strand 335
One face looks out from all his canvases 465
Others have pleasantness and praise 428
our journey was brief, it's true 43
Out of the dusk of distant woods 128
Over the land freckled with snow half-thawed 82
Over the mountains 235

Pack, clouds away! and welcome day! 227
Pray steal me not; I'm Mrs Dingley's 425
Pussy can sit by the fire and sing 474

Rose-cheekt *Lawra*, come 116

Said the Duck to the Kangaroo 52–3
Seven buxom women abreast, and arm in arm 48
Seventeen years ago you said 336
Shake hands, we shall never be friends, all's over 419
Shall I compare thee to a summer's day 175
She walks in beauty, like the night 318
She was a Phantom of delight 188–9
She wore a 'terra-cotta' dress 152
Shining in his stickiness and glistening with honey 169
Should auld acquaintance be forgot 476
Shut not so soon; the dull-ey'd night 257
Since we parted yester eve 13
Small service is true service while it lasts 289
Snowdrop of dogs, with ear of brownest dye 415
So long as we love we serve 74
Soe well I love thee, as without thee I 466
Soft falls the sweet evening 323
Somewhere there waiteth in this world of ours 357
Spring cometh in with all her hues and smells 185
Stately, kindly, lordly friend 442–4
'Stay!' said the child. The bird said, 'No 141
Strange that I did not know him then 195
Such love I cannot analyse 191
Sweet soul, do with me as thou wilt 94

Talk not of wasted affection, affection never was wasted 118
That life may be more comfortable yet 416
That morning in the presence room I stood 445
The best way to represent to life the manifold use of friendship 472
The bird a nest, the spider a web, man friendship 156
'The Bull, the Fleece are cramm'd, and not a room 258–61
The Cock is crowing 101
The daisy-button tipped wi' dew Green like the grass was sleeping 162
The dawn was apple-green 155
The English are frosty 36
The fountains mingle with the river 341
The girl I love is flesh and blood 59
The golden gift that Nature did thee geve 144
The green-house is my summer seat 269–70
The grey sea and the long black land 313
The half-seen memories of childish days 121
The lark now leaves his watery nest 319
The Lark's in the sky love 126–7
The last word this one spoke 400
The life that I have 461
The little white clouds are racing over the sky 117
The man that is open of heart to his neighbour 328
The noblest Friendship ever shewn 41
The Owl and the Pussycat went to sea 106–7
The pleasures of friendship are exquisite 311
The sea is calm tonight 210–11
The skylarks are far behind that sang over the down 198
The South wind blows open the folds of my dress 183
The spider, dropping down from twig 438
The summer down the garden walks 209
The Sun does arise 186–7
The sun has burst the sky 196
The sun used to shine while we two walked 389–90
The sunlight on the garden 217
The Swallow is a summer bird 363
The wealth of youth, we spent it well 26–7
The world had all gone wrong that day 125
The year's at the spring 87

There are two different kinds, I believe, of human attraction 91
There is a flower I wish to wear 218
There is a Garden in her face 215
There is no man, that imparteth his joys to his friend 224
There is not in the wide world a valley so sweet 307
There must have been more than just one of us 463
There's all of pleasure and all of peace 409–10
Thine eyes still shined for me, though far 274
This is the spot: – how mildly does the sun 368
Thou that hast giv'n so much to me 380–1
Though friendships differ endless in *degree* 143
Though he, that ever kind and true 212–13
Though love may be deeper, Friendship is more wide 337
Though you are in your shining days 95
Three of us afloat in the meadow by the swing 316
Time will say nothing but I told you so 20
'Tis better to sit here beside the sea 314
'Tis sweet to hear the watchdog's honest bark 343
'Tis the human touch in this world that counts 31
To me, fair friend, you never can be old 321
To night, grave sir, both my poore house, and I 347–8
Two barks met on the deep mid-sea 309–10
Two days ago with dancing glancing hair 411
Two good friends had Hiawatha 225
Two is better than one 134

Under the after-sunset sky 124
Understanding must be on both sides 179

We are all liars, because 93
We are the music-makers 248
We cannot tell the precise moment 351
We come down the green-grey jade hill 286
We have a great deal more kindness than is ever spoken 407
We have been friends together 378
We have lived and loved together 475
We met, hand to hand 296–7
We parted on the mountains, as two streams 312
We sat within the farm-house old 69–70

We talked as Girls do – 83
We talked with open heart, and tongue 303–6
We two boys together clinging 292
We were very tired, we were very merry – 285
Well – one at least is safe. One shelter'd hare 422
What I am not, and what I faine would be 383
What is this life, if full of care 268
What nature, alas! has denied 455
What virtue or what mental grace 338–9
What's the best thing in the world 204
When a friend calls to me from the road 317
When children are playing alone on the green 184
When on a summer's morn I wake 207
When the green woods laugh with the voice of joy 214
When to the sessions of sweet silent thought 431
When trouble comes your soul to try 367
When we were idlers with the loitering rills 272
When will ye think of me, my friends 23–4
When you are old and grey and full of sleep 68
Where the ash-tree weaves 25
Where the pools are bright and deep 295
Wherever I am, there's always Pooh 276–7
Who so that wisely weyes the profite and the price 119–20
Why art thou silent! Is thy love a plant 66
Why is my verse so barren of new pride 449
Why should my anxious breast repine 262
Will you come? 232–3
Wilt thou go with me sweet maid 450–1
With rue my heart is laden 302
With you first shown to me 301
Words are easy, like the wind 275
Words beget Anger: Anger brings forth blowes 464

Yes, I know that you once were my lover 200–1
You ask me 'why I like him.' Nay 92
You entered my life in a casual way 265
You have taken back the promise 72–3
You smile upon your friend to-day 379
You won't believe it. Perhaps you're too prosaic 148
Your hands lie open in the long fresh grass 190

Index of poets

Alma-Tadema, Laurence 19
Andrewes, Lancelot, Bishop of Winchester 64
Anon 29, 76, 110–11, 119–20, 125, 147, 235, 263, 477
Aristotle 197
Arnold, Sir Edwin 357
Arnold, Matthew 210–11
Auden, W. H. 20, 330

Bacon, Francis 55, 224, 245, 472
Baillie, Joanna 105
Barnes, William 253–4, 301
Barnfield, Richard 275
Barrett Browning, Elizabeth 17, 75, 137–9, 171, 204, 371
Beattie, James 199
Beddoes, Thomas Lovell 34, 415
Belloc, Hilaire 26–7
Betjeman, John 58
Binyon, Laurence 128, 219, 387
Bishop, Elizabeth 172–4
Blake, William 131, 156, 186–7, 214, 394
Boswell, James 351
Bowles, William Lisle 426
Bradstreet, Anne 446
Bridges, Robert 135–6
Brontë, Emily 441
Browne, William 360
Browning, Robert 87, 313
Bulwer-Lytton, Edward 13, 271
Burns, Robert 140, 236, 476
Byron, George Gordon, Lord 262, 280–1, 318, 343

Calverley, Charles Stuart 146
Campion, Thomas 116, 215, 290–1, 322
Carey, Henry 243–4
Chaucer, Geoffrey 429
Chesterton, G. K. 251–2
Cicero, Marcus Tullius 234
Clare, John 25, 45, 59, 126–7, 149–50, 162, 185, 205, 230–1, 242, 250, 323, 329, 427, 450–1
Clough, Arthur Hugh 38, 91

Coleridge, Hartley 272, 312
Coleridge, Mary 89
Coleridge, Samuel Taylor 143
Collins, Mortimer 71
Congreve, William 39
Cope, Wendy 104
Cowley, Abraham 420
Cowper, William 41, 98, 269–70, 338–9, 422, 455
Craik, Dinah 99

Dante Alighieri 56
Davenant, Sir William 319
Davies, Mary Carolyn 460
Davies, W. H. 207, 268
Dawson, Grace Stricker 265
de Vere, Aubrey Thomas 121
Denham, Sir John 193
Dickens, Charles 399
Dickinson, Emily 44, 51, 83, 229, 362, 406, 467
Dobson, Austin 100, 405
Donne, John 22
Drayton, Michael 466
Drinkwater, John 81
Dunbar, Paul Laurence 21, 314
Dunn, Douglas 148, 340, 463

Eliot, George 14
Eliot, T. S. 447–8
Emerson, Ralph Waldo 65, 274, 332, 407, 434

Finch, Anne, Countess of Winchelsea 273
Free, Spencer Michael 31
Frost, Robert 317

Gibran, Kahlil 375–6, 414
Graves, Robert 278, 287
Grimald, Nicholas 60, 239
Guest, Edgar 372, 462
Gurney, Ivor 412

Hale, Sarah Josepha 142
Hardy, Thomas 48, 152, 206, 237
Haynes, Carol 457

Hemans, Felicia 23–4, 309–10
Herbert, George 380–1
Herrick, Robert 42, 67, 114, 257, 267, 398, 418, 464
Heywood, Thomas 227
Hoban, Russell 169
Hogg, James 295
Holmes, Oliver Wendell 61–3, 298–300
Hood, Thomas 255
Hopkins, Gerard Manley 168
Horace 417
Housman, A. E. 170, 302, 373, 379, 419, 453–4, 473
Howard, Henry, Earl of Surrey 144, 358
Hunt, Leigh 35, 194

Jefferys, Charles 475
Jennings, Elizabeth 179, 191
Johnson, Samuel 401
Jonson, Ben 103, 167, 347–8, 383
Joseph, Jenny 196
Joyce, James 226

Keats, John 30, 238
King, Henry, Bishop of Chichester 96–7
King James Bible 134, 284
Kingsley, Charles 40, 151
Kipling, Rudyard 328, 433, 474
Knight, Joel 43, 115, 145

Lamb, Charles 50
Lamb, Mary 363
Landor, Walter Savage 218
Lawrence, D. H. 93, 155, 264, 293–4
Lear, Edward 52–3, 106–7, 439–40
Lee, Laurie 132
Lewis, Naomi 141
Li Po 286, 388
Longfellow, Henry Wadsworth 69–70, 118, 133, 225, 326–7, 468
Lowell, Amy 163–4, 183, 228
Lucas, Edward Verrall 92

MacCaig, Norman 400
MacDonald, George 435

MacNeice, Louis 217
Markham, Edwin 456
Marks, Leo 461
Marlowe, Christopher 181–2, 374
Masefield, John 90, 355
Meredith, Owen 13, 271
Mew, Charlotte 336
Millay, Edna St Vincent 37, 285
Miller, Alice Duer 36
Milne, A. A. 276–7
Moore, Thomas 192, 216, 307, 423–4

Nash, Ogden 176, 361
Nesbit, E. 109, 209
Nesbit, Wilbur D. 409–10
Norton, Caroline 200–1, 378

O'Shaughnessy, Arthur William Edgar 248

Parry, Joseph 452
Patmore, Coventry 159, 382, 408, 432
Peacock, Thomas Love 220–2
Philips, Katherine 54, 153–4, 288, 333–4, 377
Pomfret, John 416
Pope, Alexander 130
Proctor, Adelaide 72–3

Robinson, Corinne Roosevelt 337
Robinson, Edwin Arlington 195, 384
Ross, Alan 247
Rossetti, Christina 157, 296–7, 331, 359, 385, 411, 430, 458–9, 465
Rossetti, Dante Gabriel 190
Rowe, Nicholas 352

Service, Robert 392
Shakespeare, William 49, 175, 321, 431, 449
Sheffield, John, Duke of Buckingham 18
Shelley, Percy Bysshe 12, 77–9, 108, 341
Sidney, Sir Philip 246
Simcox, George Augustus 428
Smart, Christopher 349–50
Smith, Charlotte 256

Smith, Stevie 311
Southwell, Robert 32–3
Spenser, Edmund 335
Stevenson, Robert Louis 74, 184, 212–13, 316, 393, 421
Swift, Jonathan 425
Swinburne, Algernon Charles 16, 442–4

Taylor, Sir Henry 413
Tennyson, Alfred, Lord 57, 94, 177–8, 208, 258–61, 342, 353–4, 366, 445
Thomas, Edward 82, 124, 198, 232–3, 389–90
Thomson, James 86
Thoreau, Henry David 315, 344–6
Timrod, Henry 356
Twain, Mark 102, 158

van Dyke, Henry 88, 279, 397

Wagstaff, Blanche Shoemaker 320
Waller, Edmund 223
Watson, Sir William 266
Watts, Isaac 404
White, E. B. 438
Whitman, Walt 80, 292, 386
Whittier, John Greenleaf 15, 129, 165–6
Whur, Cornelius 395–6
Wilbye, John 391
Wilde, Oscar 117
Williams, B. Y. 367
Wordsworth, William 66, 101, 112–13, 180, 188–9, 249, 289, 303–6, 368, 470–1
Wyatt, Thomas 28

Yeats, W. B. 68, 95, 369–70, 469
Young, Andrew 308

Acknowledgements

W H Auden, 'If I Could Tell You' and 'As I Walked out one Evening', from *Collected Shorter Poems 1927–1957*, Faber, 1966. Reprinted with permission of Curtis Brown USA.

Hilaire Belloc, 'DEDICATORY ODE' from *Complete Verse*, reprinted by permission of Peters Fraser & Dunlop (www.petersfraserdunlop.com) on behalf of the Estate of Hilaire Belloc.

Elizabeth Bishop, 'Invitation to Miss Marianne Moore' from *Complete Poems 1927–1979*, Chatto & Windus, 1983. Reprinted with permission of Penguin Random House.

Wendy Cope, 'The Orange' (© Wendy Cope, 1992) is printed by permission of United Agents (www.unitedagents.co.uk) on behalf of Wendy Cope.

Douglas Dunn, 'You', 'Love Poem', 'Friendship of Young Poets'. Copyright © 2003, renewed. Reprinted by permission of Charles Walker/United Agents.

T S Eliot, 'Portrait of a Lady' from *Collected Poems*, Faber, 1937. Reprinted with permission of Faber & Faber.

Robin Flower, 'Pangur Ban' from *101 Happy Poems*, Faber, 2001. Reprinted with permission of Faber & Faber.

Robert Frost, 'A Time to Talk' from *Complete Poems*, Jonathan Cape, 1951. Reprinted with permission of Penguin Random House.

Robert Graves, 'Love without Hope' from *Poems Selected by Himself*, Penguin, 1961. Reprinted by permission of Carcanet Press Limited

Robert Graves, 'Two Fusiliers' from *The Penguin Book of First World War Poetry*, Penguin, 2006. Reprinted by permission of Carcanet Press Limited.

Russell Hoban, THE FRIENDLY CINNAMON BUN from THE PEDALLING MAN AND OTHER POEMS, Heinemann, by kind permission of David Higham Associates Ltd.

Horace, 'To an Old Comrade in the Army of Brutus' from *Bartlett's Poems for Occasions*, Little Brown & Co, 2004. Reprinted with permission of Little Brown.

Elizabeth Jennings, FRIENDSHIP from THE COLLECTED POEMS, Carcanet Press, by kind permission of David Higham Associates Ltd.

Jenny Joseph, 'The Sun has Burst the Sky' from *Rose in Afternoon and Other Poems*, Dent, 1973.
Reprinted with permission of Johnson + Alcock.

Joel Knight, 'Brave and Glorious', 'Tea with Laura', 'On the Fifth Floor in "Montmartre"'. With kind permission of Joel Knight.

Laurie Lee, 'April Rise' from *Poets of Our Time, John Murray,* 1965.Reprinted with permission of Curtis Brown.

Leo Marks, 'The Life That I Have' from *Between Silk & Cyanide: The Story of SOE's Code War,* 1998. Reprinted by permission of HarperCollins Publishers Ltd

Norman MacCaig, 'Two Friends' from *Collected Poems*, Chatto & Windus, 1990. Reproduced with permission of the Licensor through PLSclear.

Louis MacNeice, SUNSHINE IN THE GARDEN from COLLECTED POEMS, Faber & Faber, by kind permission of David Higham Associates Ltd.

John Masefield, 'The Word' and 'Being her Friend' courtesy of The Society of Authors as the Literary Representative of the Estate of John Masefield.

Edna St. Vincent Millay, 'Love is not all: it is not meat nor drink' from *Collected Poems*. Copyright 1931, © 1958 by Edna St. Vincent Millay and Norma Millay Ellis. Used with the permission of The Permissions Company LLC, on behalf of Holly Peppe, Literary Executor, The Edna St. Vincent Millay Society, www.millay.org.

A A Milne, 'Us Two' from *Now We Are Six*. Reprinted with permission of Curtis Brown.

Ogden Nash, 'Compliments of a Friend' and 'Reprise' copyright © 1949, renewed. Reprinted by permission of Curtis Brown, Ltd.

Alan Ross, 'Test Match at Lords' from *To Whom it May Concern: New Poems 1952–7*, Hamish Hamilton, 1958. Reprinted with permission of Alan Ross.

Robert Service, 'The Tramps' from *Collected Verse vol I*, Ernest Benn Ltd, 1930. Reprinted with permission of William Krasilovsky.

Stevie Smith, 'The Pleasures of Friendship' from *Collected Poems*, Allan Lane, 1975. Reprinted with permission of Faber & Faber.

Andrew Young, 'Beauty and Love' from *Complete Poems*, Secker & Warburg, 1974. Reprinted with permission of Ruth Lowbury

Pavilion Books is committed to respecting the intellectual property rights of others. We have therefore taken all reasonable efforts to ensure that the reproduction of all contents on these pages is done with the full consent of the copyright owners. If you are aware of unintentional omissions, please contact the company directly so that any necessary corrections may be made for future editions.

Firstly, huge thanks to everyone at Hatchards for looking after my books so well. Thanks to Jeremy Bourne, Sue and David Gibb, Louy Piachaud, Ian Prince and Kaaren Ramus for suggesting poems, Joel Knight for writing them and Francis Cleverdon for advice. Nicola Newman and Tina Persaud were brilliant editors and my agent Teresa Chris was as invaluable as ever. The Saison Poetry Library on the South Bank is a wonderful place to work and the staff were all amazing at sourcing obscure poems. Finally thanks to Matilda, the perfect paperweight, and love to Mat and Sarah.